We Before Me

We Before Me

THE ADVANTAGE OF PUTTING OTHERS BEFORE SELF

Mark E. Green, M.D.

SALEM
BOOKS

an imprint of Regnery Publishing
Washington, D.C.

Salem Books™ is a trademark of Salem Communications Holding Corporation. Regnery® and its colophon are registered trademarks of Salem Communications Holding Corporation.

Cataloging-in-Publication data on file with the Library of Congress.

ISBN: 978-1-68451-522-6
eISBN: 978-1-68451-576-9

Published in the United States by Salem Books
An Imprint of Regnery Publishing
A Division of Salem Media Group
Washington, D.C.
www.SalemBooks.com

10 9 8 7 6 5 4 3 2 1

Books are available in quantity for promotional or premium use. For information on discounts and terms, please visit our website: www.SalemBooks.com

To Camie.

Thanks for thirty-five years of life together
and for modeling "we before me" to the world.

CONTENTS

Foreword

Mark Green is a remarkable man who doesn't think he's remarkable. That is what I love about him. His book reflects who he is. It is genuine. It is understated. It is filled with truth.

What is particularly surprising about *We Before Me* is the beauty of its stories and the powerful simplicity of its message. It is astonishing that it is written by a politician, but Mark doesn't consider himself to be a politician. He is just a representative of people who want what is true, good, and beautiful.

More than anything else, this book is a remedy, a blueprint for our nation's recovery and revival. But it is not focused on economic or foreign policy, or on policy at all. It is about the character that is necessary for the people in a nation that wants to thrive. As the founders of our nation knew, it requires faith, integrity, and sacrifice—all things that Mark understands and embodies.

Though I'd like every American to read this book, I realize that is not a realistic expectation. But it is worth saying that *if* every citizen of this nation were to ingest and internalize the stories and messages in *We Before Me*, the country would be a drastically better place for everyone, regardless of their political affiliation or socioeconomic circumstances.

And that is the point. We are one nation, one people, guided by one truth. And the pursuit of that truth requires selflessness.

—Patrick Lencioni,
author of *The Five Dysfunctions of a Team*

Introduction

T his was their finest hour.

In Great Britain's darkest days, when the island nation stood practically alone against a terrifying Nazi war machine that had already overrun much of Western Europe, Prime Minister Winston Churchill uttered those words to inspire and strengthen the resolve of the British people.

Churchill addressed the House of Commons and the nation on June 18, 1940, at a grim moment of national crisis. France had just fallen to Germany. Nothing but the narrow English Channel stood between Britain and imminent invasion. In a few short weeks, bombs would be falling on London, and everyone knew it. In the conclusion to this iconic address, the great statesman sugarcoated nothing, but plainly laid out the nightmarish implications of failing to rise to the challenge of the times.

What General Weygand has called the Battle of France is over...the Battle of Britain is about to begin. Upon this battle depends the survival of Christian civilization. Upon it depends our own British life, and the long continuity of our institutions and our Empire. The whole fury and might of the enemy must very soon be turned on us. Hitler knows that he will have to break us in this island or lose the war.

If we can stand up to him, all Europe may be freed, and the life of the world may move forward into broad, sunlit uplands.

But if we fail, then the whole world, including the United States, including all that we have known and cared for, will sink into the abyss of a new dark age made more sinister, and perhaps more protracted, by the lights of perverted science.

Let us therefore brace ourselves to our duties, and so bear ourselves, that if the British Empire and its Commonwealth last for a thousand years, men will still say, "This was their finest hour."[1]

Their finest hour. Please notice that Churchill appealed not to the individual self-interest of his countrymen. Instead, he appealed to their sense of collective identity. He called for courage and sacrifice, and asked that those monumental sacrifices be made not only for oneself and one's immediate family and neighbors, but for the people in the next village, for every subject of the British Crown in distant corners of the earth, for all of Europe, and even for other freedom-loving peoples like the Americans.

In other words, Churchill understood the power of the principle on which this book is based and which serves as its title: *We Before Me*. Churchill knew that if his nation was to summon the necessary strength, courage, resolve, and ingenuity to defeat Nazi Germany, everyone had to be willing to selflessly sacrifice for the common good.

Unlike Great Britain in 1940, our greatest threat is not an external enemy bent on conquest, although those exist. No, our mortal threat has arisen from within our own borders. That enemy is extreme polarization. We're a nation divided at levels not seen since the Civil War. There is a real question whether the United States of America can remain the freest, most prosperous, most blessed nation the planet has ever seen. Beyond the broad historical divisions of North and South, urban and rural, Republican and Democrat, liberal and conservative, the fault lines of our nation's current conflict run through every region, city, and neighborhood, and even divide the middle of some households. We've been shouting past each other for a couple of decades. We've developed a knee-jerk habit of demonizing those who see things differently. Now we're tearing ourselves apart at the granular level.

Some noticed the first hairline cracks in this seismic rift emerging shortly after the *Roe v. Wade* decision of 1973. Prior to that ruling, each of the fifty states—what late Supreme Court Justice Louis Brandeis called the "laboratories of democracy"—was in the midst of the difficult but essential process of finding solutions to the complex challenge of abortion. Each was searching for a legal way to resolve the delicate civil/human rights issue in a manner that most of its citizens could support in good conscience. *Roe* ripped that vital process from the hands of the people and their state representatives and brought it to an abrupt end. What followed were decades of conflict and strife at every level of our society, and that conflict continues unabated to this day. The violence targeting pro-life women's counseling centers and churches following the leak and official announcement of the 2022 U.S. Supreme Court decision that overturned *Roe* underscores the point.

Other observers, in trying to identify the moment our national discourse went off the rails of civility, point to the nasty battle over President Ronald Reagan nominating Judge Robert Bork to the United States Supreme Court in 1987. Indeed, a case can be made that the success of the nationwide smear campaign against Bork incentivized and inspired an entire generation of activists. The incident turned the distinguished intellectual's name into a verb, resulting in future attempts to "bork" every Republican president's Supreme Court nominations, up to and including those of Brett Kavanaugh and Amy Coney Barrett in 2018 and 2020, respectively. But the intensity and viciousness of these battles was largely rooted in the desire to protect *Roe v. Wade*. Whereas people living in the late 1800s often called the American Civil War "the war between the states," the ongoing rift in America over the abortion issue has been called "the war within the states."[2]

But the societal divide over abortion is only one facet of a conflict that has steadily eroded our national sense of common values in recent decades. At the same time, we've witnessed the steady disintegration of the unique American version of the social contract with our neighbors and fellow citizens, rooted in the Golden Rule of Judeo-Christianity. Increasingly fewer of us were raised with a moral code that simply encourages us to treat others as we wish to be treated.

Along the way, many of us seem to have forgotten how to empathize with anyone with a different perspective, how to civilly disagree, how to argue in good faith, how to impute good faith to our opponents, or even how to have cordial relationships with people who don't hold our views. The problem is not just that our political discourse has turned toxic and ugly—although, as a third-term congressman on Capitol Hill, I can say that is certainly has. No, our watercoolers, the grocery store checkout lines, and the stands at the youth soccer fields have too often become battle zones filled with rancor and hostility. No corner of American life is spared. Just ask Congressman Steve Scalise, who nearly died in 2017 when an assailant fired on Republicans practicing for the annual Congressional Baseball Game for Charity. There seems to be no refuge from the conflict.

A 2019 article in *The Spectator* captured the tenor of our day with its title, "The Gilded Rage: Why Is America So Angry?" The author, Peter Wood, is well known for his 2006 book, *A Bee in the Mouth: Anger in America Now.* Wood concludes his *Spectator* essay by saying:

> For too many Americans, anger has become the default emotion.... Proud-of-itself anger is now, unfortunately, a dominating presence in our national life: a permission slip to treat others rudely and to spew contempt on the innocent if we believe we are acting on some higher principle such as "social justice."[3]

Unchecked, chronic anger tends to lead to action—and now we see that anger metastasizing into violence and destruction. Stores burned and looted. Business owners fleeing Seattle and Chicago, and downtown areas boarded up in cities across the country. Public monuments torn down. Beautiful public spaces defaced with obscene graffiti. Citizens sucker-punched simply for looking too Jewish—or too anything—as they walk down the street.

Just as alarming, many prominent respected voices in the pillar institutions of our society—education, the media, and government—make excuses for that violence. Some defend it. Some applaud it. More than a few openly encourage it.

Fueling and accelerating this rift are two forces. One is quite new; the other is as ancient as mankind itself.

The more recent force is the rise of digital communication, social media in particular. First, it was email and texting. The loss of face-to-face or voice communications allowed people to say things they would never say in person. Over time, it became easier for people to be increasingly offensive and rude, to say things they previously would have suppressed. Social media took that behavior to the next level. Further, the emergence of the smartphone put news and opinions in our hands every minute of our waking hours. If something terrible happens somewhere in the world, we can all see video of it on our phones within minutes. We now witness catastrophes and atrocities unfold in real time, and we share them with all our online connections.

This phenomenon has warped our view of the world and our nation. We've become convinced that we live in a much darker, more sinister and unjust place than we actually do. The entire online enterprise runs on "clicks" and pageviews. Attention is how everyone gets paid. Sadly, the best way to get attention is to incite masses to either fear or outrage. As a result of the content we consume, most of us live in a constant state of combined rage and alarm. Our hardwired, fight-or-flight response mechanisms never shut off.

On top of that, the advent of social media empowered us to filter the information we receive so that it aligns only with our views and what we want to believe. We can mute, unfollow, and block all messaging that opposes what we already think. Psychologists long ago identified something called "confirmation bias"[4]—our brains' tendency to readily note events that line up with our existing beliefs and to be somewhat blind to those that would contradict them. As a result, we're constantly noticing things that validate our preferred narrative and ignoring everything that doesn't.

To be sure, it feels good to have a high-profile person or someone with credentials validate your views. None of us are immune to this seductive lure; it's a little like a drug. And 24/7 digital connectivity allows this good feeling to become an addiction. Once addicted, it becomes impossible to see or hear contrary information without responding to it with anger or fear.

But this is only one of two forces ripping the fabric of our society to pieces. The more ancient monster I referred to above is one of mankind's most primal and destructive instincts: tribalism.

Cain, the world's first farmer, resented and ultimately killed his brother Abel, the world's first livestock herder. People have been dividing into warring groups ever since. To this day, tribal identity still drives economics and politics in many parts of the world. As a soldier, I saw it firsthand in Afghanistan, Iraq, and several other war-ravaged places.

One of the most remarkable accomplishments of Western civilization—or to use Churchill's term, "Christian civilization"—is breaking down social tribalism. The American experiment has been especially successful in creating a unified, common culture out of people from every imaginable background. For more than 230 years, our remarkable melting pot has incorporated and assimilated individuals from every corner of the world. And, historically, the rigid class distinctions that distinguished many immigrants' points of origin seem to dissolve on American soil. "Social mobility" has characterized our system.

By this I mean that in most cultures, historically and today, one's birth determines his station in life. Whatever class or caste one's parents belong to becomes the one they inhabit their entire life, and the same is true for their children. But throughout most of our nation's history, people born into abject poverty have been able to rise into the middle class, and even achieve extraordinary wealth, through hard work, initiative, and creativity. The rags-to-riches Horatio Alger stories have become clichéd in our culture for a reason: People who work hard to achieve a better station in life succeed all the time in America. And the reverse has always been the case as well. That is, a person born to great wealth and privilege can—through laziness, foolishness, and good old-fashioned stupidity—be reduced to poverty. Social mobility runs both ways.

Yet our emerging tribalism now threatens our beautiful legacy of freedom and opportunity. In her 2018 book, *Political Tribes: Group Instinct and the Fate of Nations*, legal scholar Amy Chua explains why tribalism is so seductive and represents such a threat to our legacy:

> The great Enlightenment principles of modernity—liberalism, secularism, rationality, equality, free markets—do not provide the kind of tribal group identity that human beings crave and have always craved. They have strengthened individual rights and individual liberty, created unprecedented opportunity and prosperity, transformed human consciousness, but they speak to people as individuals and as members of the human race, whereas the tribal instinct occupies the realm in between.[5]

The rapidly increasing tribalism we've seen over the last few years show Chua's words to be prophetic. She pointed to America's legacy of providing social unity and identity for a huge variety of individuals and described our nation as a "super-group" rather than merely an assemblage of competing "tribes." She sounded the alarm that our nation was in danger of throwing away that extraordinary distinction, and that we were teetering on the edge of something more primal.

> America's continued existence as a super-group is under tremendous strain today. America is beginning to display destructive political dynamics much more typical of developing and non-Western countries: ethnonationalist movements; backlash by elites against the masses; popular backlash against both "the establishment" and "outsider minorities" viewed as disproportionately powerful;

and, above all, the transformation of democracy into an engine of zero-sum political tribalism.[6]

In 2020, the "strain" on America's social fabric began to reach the breaking point under the combined pressures of the COVID-19 pandemic, a contentious presidential election, and the ascendance of identity politics—another face of the tribalism Chua warned us about—as the dominant paradigm among younger Americans. So why has it taken hold so quickly over the last few decades? Writer Jonah Goldberg points to the secularization of our culture:

> Humans must believe in something. They need a story of themselves and their place in the world. When traditional religion, morality, and the institutions of civil society—all of which place important constraints on human behavior by channeling ambition in productive ways—recede or vanish, we do not rely on pure reason as our lodestar. Human nature, like nature generally, rushes in to fill the void.[7]

This is exactly right. And human nature left to itself, as the last six thousand years of civilizational history testifies, is capable of some truly ugly things. As this book unfolds, you'll learn that I've been an eyewitness to some of those ugly things humans are capable of when they abandon our higher unifying values and surrender to selfish tribalism. I spent a night peeking into the dark soul of the "Butcher of Baghdad," Saddam Hussein. At the same time, I've also had the privilege of witnessing people at their most noble and self-sacrificial, and I've had a front row seat for extraordinary acts of courage.

In writing this book, I am not suggesting we all have to agree. The issues before us are critical and sometimes emotional. It is difficult, for example, for some people to choose between the hard-drawn positions of "it's a baby" or "it's a woman's body" when discussing abortion. We need to listen to each other and treat people with different views as fellow Americans.

I write to call us back from the brink—to mark a proven pathway that leads us as a nation back to a place of freedom and opportunity for all, irrespective of race, class, or circumstances of birth. I write because I'm convinced it's not too late.

The precepts and principles I'm about to lay out will not only work to make our nation more sustainable, stable, and prosperous, but they will do the same for you as an individual. These principles represent a roadmap to a life well-lived and prove just as powerful when applied to a business, a nonprofit organization, a church, or a family.

In this book, I lean heavily on my own life experiences because they are what I know best. I don't think I'm exaggerating when I say my journey has been an unusual one, but you can judge that for yourself. Today, it's my privilege to represent the wonderful people of Tennessee's Seventh District in the United States Congress. That, in itself, is an unlikely outcome for a boy who grew up on a dirt road in rural southern Mississippi, with a disabled father who was scratching out a blue-collar living.

After high school, I found myself a cadet at the United States Military Academy at West Point, proudly becoming a part of "the long gray line" of men and women who marched on that storied parade ground. After graduating with a degree in quantitative business management (concentrating in economics), I began my service in the Army infantry, went on to U.S. Army Ranger School, and ultimately served as a commander in the 82nd Airborne Division. I ended up in medical school and with a residency in emergency medicine while still serving in the military, which led to my serving as the flight surgeon for several of our nation's Tier One Special Operations Forces on missions in Afghanistan and Iraq. As I've already mentioned, one of these missions resulted in the capture of Saddam Hussein. I'll share some insights and lessons gleaned from an hours-long conversation with him during his first night in U.S. custody.

Although some of my personal recollections will serve to illustrate the principles, precepts, and pathways that lead to renewal, please know that this book is not about me. It's about "we." That's why I'm compelled to share what I've learned from a life that has put me in a position to observe the very worst and the very best of us. As I do, I will speak often of my Christian faith. It is very important to me and has shaped me in more ways than I can describe. I simply cannot tell my story any other way. It is also important for me to stress to everyone that I am no saint. I did my best and made my mistakes, but my faith is the target on the wall. As an old mentor once told me, "If you aim at nothing, you hit it every time." Frankly, my best lessons were learned with my foot planted firmly in my mouth or my face in the dirt. And, for reasons I'll explain as we go, it is essential that we, as a people, come to some sort of broad consensus about what constitutes right and wrong, and about virtue—what some have called a "moral code."

Most of all, I am compelled to write because, like Great Britain in 1940, we, too, are a nation facing a life-and-death crisis. My diagnosis is that we have a grave societal illness. The balance of this book represents the time-tested prescription for curing this potentially fatal set of conditions before it's too late.

Will future generations of Americans look back at those of us experiencing the trials and tests of this perilous moment in history and say, "This was their finest hour"? That is my hope, and it's the purpose of this book. Let's get started.

CHAPTER 1

We Before Me
A Heritage

James, earn this. Earn it.

—dying words of Captain Miller,
Saving Private Ryan

What have I gotten myself into?

That was the thought that briefly seized my mind as I unexpectedly walked into a somber memorial service for fallen soldiers. In that moment, my general sense of excitement and anticipation suddenly took a 180-degree turn into a zone of sober reflection.

The year was 2002. I was fulfilling a long-held goal of joining one of America's elite special operations units: the Night Stalkers of the 160th Special Operations Aviation Regiment (SOAR).

I had graduated from U.S. Army Ranger School in 1987, and back then, many considered that alone enough to be called an Army Ranger. I, however, did not. I considered myself to be a "Ranger qualified" officer, but to be a Ranger, you had to have worn the scroll—the unit patch indicating you were assigned to a Ranger unit.

All Army infantry officers are sent to the Army Ranger School at
Fort Benning, Georgia—a rigorous rite of passage. About 70 percent
do not make it through this arduous course. When I was in the Army,
that 70 percent was considered only partially trained. I was proud of
having finished it, but I still wanted that scroll. In time, after deploying
as the doctor in support of Ranger and other elite units in combat as
a part of special operations task forces and caring for those wounded
in battle, my friends who served in the Ranger Regiment would begin
calling me a Ranger. I was honored when they did so.[1]

I loved Ranger School because I had wanted to test myself
alongside—and against—the best. It teaches you how to lead when
you and the individuals in your unit are starving, exhausted, and sleep
deprived. It demands putting "we before me" to help your buddy get
his "go" on patrols, and to do this when your body is essentially
digesting itself in order to stay alive. (I weighed 180 pounds when I
started the course and 158 when I finished.) To succeed, I'd had to put
my Ranger buddy ahead of myself. He had done the same, and we
had gotten our Ranger tabs. What's more, I had grown up seeing the
"we before me" ethic modeled daily in my home. And at West Point,
I had learned the history of the "long gray line" I would become a
small part of—a history filled with honor, duty, self-sacrifice, and love
of neighbor. These are the essence of "we before me."

So, on this important day, I proudly reported for duty at Fort
Campbell, Kentucky, to sign in with the Night Stalkers. This unit was,
and still is, the primary rotary-wing (helicopter) group tasked with
supporting all Department of Defense Special Operations Forces. As
such, it is one of the most secretive and select special operations units
in the Army.

That secrecy was very evident on the day I arrived. The Night
Stalkers headquarters is essentially an ultra-secure compound within
a secure compound; the levels of security I had to pass just to sign in

only added to my already-heightened sense of excitement and anticipation. I knew the history of the group I was joining. The 160th was born of hard lessons drawn from tragedy and frustration: Created in the wake of mistakes made during the high-risk effort to rescue fifty-two American hostages being held in Tehran, Iran, by Islamic militants in April 1980, the 160th pioneered night-flying techniques and tactics for moving specialized teams into high-risk, high-threat areas in extreme conditions, with surgical precision, and under cover of darkness, to ensure they would never be made again.

I'd watched Operation Urgent Fury in Grenada with interest, and more than a little envy, when the Night Stalkers saw their first combat operations in 1983. I'd also watched from a distance Operation Just Cause, the 1989 mission to depose Panamanian dictator Manuel Noriega. Again, the Night Stalkers served as "the tip of the spear," rescuing an American citizen from a prison guarded by Noriega's henchmen.

A short time later, I had been filled with the strange mixture of pride and sorrow that only soldiers know when, in October 1993, at the request of President Bill Clinton, the 160th deployed on a mission to Somalia in support of United Nations efforts to provide food to the starving in that war-torn nation, then engaged in an eighteen-hour firefight against hostiles who vastly outnumbered them. The battle, now known as the Battle of Mogadishu and immortalized by the book and movie *Black Hawk Down*, involved fighting at an intensity U.S. forces had not seen since Vietnam. Five Night Stalkers were killed, and eight aircraft were either damaged or destroyed—but the enemy casualties were estimated to be between 350 and two thousand. The valor, heroism, and self-sacrifice our troops exhibited in that incident epitomize the "we before me" spirit I hope to explain throughout this book.

I had graduated from West Point in 1986, followed by nine years as an Army infantry officer and numerous other special training schools; I then graduated near the top of my medical school class in 1999, and then from the best emergency medicine program nation-wide in 2002. And now, here I was, back on a military base to join the best of the best—but there in front of me was a stark reminder of the worst that can happen.

As I surveyed the memorial service into which I had stumbled, the faces of young and thirty-something wives, some with black veils, stood out. Their children stood in somber silence. All their husbands and fathers had just paid the ultimate price of "we before me."

A somber officer was addressing them. Behind him, three charcoal-gray slabs of granite stood upright. The center slab carried the following words in big, bold letters:

IN MEMORY OF FALLEN NIGHT STALKERS
"NIGHT STALKERS DON'T QUIT"

This was the Night Stalkers' Memorial Wall—the monument honoring the combat dead of the 160th SOAR. In my excitement over signing in, I'd completely forgotten that day's date: September 11, 2002, the first anniversary of the worst attack on American soil since Pearl Harbor.

As I approached the gathering as inconspicuously as possible, I could hear the presiding officer announcing the names of the Night Stalkers who had died in the past year fighting the war on terror—nine in all. One year into Operation Enduring Freedom, the Night Stalker losses were greater than those of any other unit in the Army. And I was standing with their families—wives, children, mothers, fathers. I was on hallowed ground.

I was thirty-seven years old, a husband, and the father of two small children. I had more to lose than ever before in my life. More accurately, my wife, Camie, and kids had more to lose. And there was no question that joining this organization would bring me close to the fight. Camie and I had discussed that reality at length many times as we pondered and prayed about the decision. Ultimately, we were both at peace and in agreement. This was what I had wanted throughout my military career. What's more, it seemed everything I'd done and experienced up to that point was all in preparation for this challenge. Nevertheless, it was a stunning "coincidence" that I should arrive at Night Stalkers headquarters at that precise moment.

Yet, as a Christian, I don't really believe in coincidences. I believe everything in my life is infused with God's providence. The Bible is replete with verses that affirm this, like Proverbs 16:33: "The lot is cast into the lap, but its every decision is from the LORD" (CSB). Random chance does not control our lives; God has a say. So my initial, startled thought of *What have I gotten myself into?* eventually changed to, *God, why did You put me here at this point in time?*

As I pondered that question, an Army chaplain rose, speaking words of comfort, hope, and strength—a message like those I'd heard many times in church when I was growing up in rural Mississippi. Suddenly, I felt a wave of gratitude wash over me for a military culture that hadn't banished faith or relegated talk of God to quiet whispers in private places only.

Clearly, not every soldier is a Christian or even religious. But at that time, active-duty military circles still exemplified freedom *of* religion, rather than freedom *from* religion. One of the reasons that is important is that military families experience stresses, hazards, and losses at levels few civilians can understand. Surveys of soldiers reveal that for most, faith provides an anchor for the soul that enables them to endure hardship and pain. For many, it is also a firewall against survivor's guilt and the pain of having to violate their spirits by taking another person's life—something psychiatrists call "moral injury."

On that day, the chaplain's stirring words and well-chosen Scripture passages did more than move me: They reminded me where I first learned the power and importance of "we before me."

■ ■ ■

I first discovered the phrase "we before me" sewn into SOAR baseball caps soon after arriving to the unit, yet I had been learning its basic principles all my life.

My parents modeled that lifestyle in front of my siblings and me. Their lives were about selflessness, sacrifice, and serving others. We've all heard the maxim that some things are "more caught than taught." There is a lot of truth to that. However, my parents both modeled *and* taught the "we before me" ethic, and much of that teaching came from the Bible, particularly the parables and sayings of Jesus.

In the Sermon on the Mount, Jesus lays out the importance of going the extra mile when others ask for help. In the parable of the good Samaritan, a cultural outcast goes out of his way to rescue and restore a person who might not have given him the time of day.

You may have come across the term "servant leadership" in a business or management book. However, you may not know that the concept is rooted in something Jesus told His followers—namely, that anyone aspiring to be the greatest should do so by becoming the servant of all (see Matthew 23:11). On another occasion, Jesus said, speaking of Himself: "For even the Son of Man did not come to be served, but to serve, and to give His life a ransom for many" (Mark 10:45 NKJV). And in the days before His death, He told His disciples, "Greater love hath no man than this, that a man lay down his life for his friends" (John 15:13 KJ21). This, of course, was Christ's purpose: to lay down His life to pay man's debt of sin and reconcile him back into a relationship with the Creator God.

Likewise, the Apostle Paul wrote powerfully about how a community is like the human body: All its various and diverse parts are vital and have a key role to play (see 1 Corinthians 12:12–27). Paul points out that it would be self-destructive madness for one body part to say to another, "I don't need you." My mother frequently emphasized this metaphor as I grew up. The point was all of us have been given gifts and abilities, and a responsibility to use them for the good of the whole.

The Bible is filled with statements that point to the nobility and world-changing power of putting others first and the needs of the team above one's personal agenda.

These lessons served me well when I arrived at the United States Military Academy at West Point, New York, right out of high school. As an incoming fourth-class cadet, a freshman, you learn immediately that you are part of a team, and the group's success is what matters most. There, the principle of "we before me" is literally "drilled" into you, and for good reason: In battle, functioning as a cohesive, selfless team often makes the difference between victory and defeat, life and death.

It's impossible to stand on the Plain—the historic central parade ground—at West Point and not think about the extraordinary people who walked that sod in the academy's two-plus centuries of existence. The site, literally a point of land jutting out into the Hudson River from its west bank, was first used by the Continental Army in 1778 before being turned into a training ground for soldiers in 1794. Those soldiers, and all who followed after the formation of the United States Military Academy in 1802, comprise what has been called "the long gray line" of men (and, since 1976, women) who have donned that heather uniform: presidents, scores of four-star generals, U.S. senators, cabinet officers, astronauts, business founders, CEOs, university presidents, and a long list of war heroes. Iconic names like Eisenhower, MacArthur, Pershing, Patton, Custer, Grant, Aldrin, and so many others featured prominently on the pages of our history books stood on that Plain. In fact, my class of 1986 produced a Secretary of State, a Secretary of Defense, a CIA director, two U.S. congressmen, one Vice Chief of Staff of the Army, and a host of CEOs, state legislators, and university deans and presidents. There is a favorite saying among the history instructors at West Point: "Much of the history we teach was made by people we taught."[2] This is no exaggeration. A general once welcomed an arriving class of "plebes" with an address that said, "The history of the United States of America, and the history of the United States Army, and the history of the United States Military Academy are so closely intertwined as to be inextricable, one from the other. As goes the Army, so goes the nation."[3]

At the academy, you quickly learn that the phrase "the long gray line" describes the very real, yet invisible connection that binds every West Point graduate to every man and woman who came before, and to and all those who will come after. The phrase comes from a stanza in the Academy's official hymn, "The Corps":

The long gray line of us stretches,
thro' the years of a century told.
And the last man feels to his marrow,
the grip of your far-off hold.

That "far-off hold" is real. You feel it when you put on that uniform and when you walk the halls. *The Long Gray Line* is also the title of a 1989 Pulitzer Prize-winning book by Rick Atkinson, which documented the lives and achievements of a single extraordinary West Point class, the class of 1966, which entered active military service just as American involvement in the war in Vietnam was approaching its peak. Each West Point class chooses a motto. The class of 1966 chose "We Before Me."

Nowhere is the "we before me" ethic more poignantly evident than in one particular aspect of the Army Ranger code of honor, which every graduate has memorized: "I will never leave a fallen comrade to fall into the hands of the enemy." This is often paraphrased as "leave no man behind." This ethic is shared by many other branches of the U.S. armed forces. Some of the most moving heroism and self-sacrifice I've personally witnessed and heard about directly was displayed while honoring this creed. A few of these incidents you may have heard about; most of them you haven't and never will. Many are known only to those who served alongside those heroes. I'll share a few throughout this book.

When I think about that Ranger Creed and "we before me," I can't help but recall the iconic movie *Saving Private Ryan*. The harrowing first twenty minutes of that film come closer to capturing the intensity and chaos of infantry combat than perhaps any movie ever made, but it is in its climactic finale that we see the Army Ranger Creed most vividly and poignantly on display: Captain Miller, a Ranger Company commander, is sent on a special mission to extract Private Ryan, whose brothers have all been killed in combat, for the sake of his Gold Star mother. Once his team finally locates Ryan, Miller informs him that he has orders to send him home. Ryan's response rings true to the spirit and character I observed many times in my military career.

> **Private Ryan:** It doesn't make any sense, sir. Why? Why do I deserve to go? Why not any of these guys? They all fought just as hard as me.
> **Captain Miller:** Is that what they're supposed to tell your mother when they send her another folded American flag?
> **Private Ryan:** Tell her that when you found me, I was here and I was with the only brothers that I have left, and that there was no way I was gonna desert them. I think she'll understand that. There's no way I'm leaving this bridge.

If you've seen the film, you already know every man on Miller's team dies getting Ryan to safety, except one. You also know that Miller is fatally wounded in a firefight at the end of the movie, and that with his last breath, he challenges Ryan to "earn this."

I suppose a lot of us who've lost friends and comrades in the line of duty suffer from what psychologists call "survivor's guilt." But I also know that a big part of what has motivated me in the years since I left the military has been something much bigger than that: I've chosen to work to keep American free, strong, united, and prosperous, because I, too, felt a challenge to earn what the selfless sacrifices of others had purchased for me.

As Americans, we all stand as part of a long line in this moment in time. Millions before us worked, sweated, bled, sacrificed, and died to bequeath to us the extraordinary gift that is America. That same line extends into the future, incorporating generations of Americans yet unborn. We, too, must embrace our responsibility and rise to the challenge of our times for their sakes.

CHAPTER 2

The Elusive Pea
"We Before Me" Helps Us Overcome Adversity

*Show me someone who has done something worth-
while, and I will show you someone who has overcome
adversity.*

—Lou Holtz

I was in the first grade when my father, whom I revered as only a
six-year-old boy can, came home with a significant piece of himself
missing: His right arm was gone. My memories of that moment are
painful but hazy. My mother tells me that it really shook me.

In the early 1970s, Dad was a machine foreman at a paper mill
near our little community of Monticello, Mississippi—population:
1,790. The paper industry was and still is a huge component of
Mississippi's economy, and Dad made a good living working as a team
leader at the plant. Even so, we lived on a dirt road outside of town,
and I suspect that most people today would assume we were poor.

I was the oldest of three kids. We grew up in a 1,400-square-foot,
three-bedroom, brick ranch-style home atop a hill with two acres of
land. My brother, Rick, and I shared bunk beds, a closet, and a room
that was about ten by eleven feet. It was all we needed. We children

fought very little, because a trip to pick out our own switch would immediately follow if we did. Just outside our back door was a large shrub whose limbs grew stiff and straight. My parents used those "switches" for spankings, and when we got older, they had us retrieve the ones they would use. If we came back with a tiny, flimsy limb that we thought might not hurt as much, they went out and picked another one, and the consequences were far worse.

Years later I realized why my dad said what he did before every spanking: "This is going to hurt me more than it's going to hurt you." It took having children, and caring enough to teach them through discipline that excellence is the minimum standard, to understand what he meant. Tough love is a central aspect of leading with a "we before me" mentality.

There is another aspect to my dad's demand for excellence. Mom frequently quoted the Bible verse, "A good name is rather to be chosen than great riches, and loving favor rather than silver and gold" (Proverbs 22:1 KJ21). Embedded in that verse is a wisdom principle: Your reputation is everything—and in a small rural town, that reputation could last for decades. Dad made it clear that as members of the Green family, we each gained from the reputation of the whole, and any one person's actions could either enhance that or harm it. He believed the whole was greater than the parts. More than anything, that defines the "we before me" creed.

"Mark Edward" was the way my dad called for me, in a building crescendo with the emphasis on "-ward." And he had to call me a lot, because if I was not doing homework, I was outside. My favorite pastime was fishing. Rick and I fished nearly every day—think of the movie *A River Runs Through It*. Many days, we brought home a mess of fish, cleaned them, and the family ate them for supper. (A "mess" of fish is an official unit of measurement in southern Mississippi that means "enough to feed your family.")

When not fishing, we were using scrap lumber to build treehouses. These were nothing elaborate, but they were our creations and often perched forty to fifty feet up in a pine tree. The only way Dad had to get us inside for supper was to yell, and for me, that was "Mark Edward!" (One time, Dad and I were walking together in town, and a man who lived more than half a mile away saw me and asked him, "Is that Mark Edward?" He must have heard my dad call me every day all the way from his house.)

Mom was a disciplinarian, too, but in a more subtle way. In high school, there was a girl in the grade behind me I was attracted to, but who had a certain kind of reputation. Mom emphatically refused to allow me to see her, deployed her spies in our small town, and with threats of taking away my car and other privileges, ultimately won the day. That girl soon became pregnant by another guy, and their indiscretion altered both of their life trajectories.

The counterbalance to my parents' harsh discipline was their practice of being amazingly complimentary and affirming of every success and victory we had as kids, particularly Dad. He bragged so enthusiastically about my every accomplishment in high school that more than one father asked his son, "Why can't you be like Mark Green?" (One high school friend pleaded with me to ask my father to stop.) Mom praised our successes, too, but balanced that with, "Let's not brag on ourselves." She often quoted the Bible verse that says, "Pride goeth before destruction, and a haughty spirit before a fall" (Proverbs 16:18 KJV). (You'll find an important "we before me" principle in that little verse.)

Arrogance is always followed by bad decision-making and negative outcomes. Ask General George Custer, who let his incredible acts of bravery and battlefield success during the Civil War go to his head. Years later, in the Montana Territory, his arrogance cost him his life and worse, the lives of all of his cavalry troopers when they fought

Native Americans in the Battle of the Little Bighorn. Arrogance clearly has no place in a "we before me" culture.

However, celebrating one's success creates a correct picture of who we are. It instills confidence that is balanced with accountability. It also reinforces the "we before me" principle that individual excellence is expected for the good of the team. Holding yourself and the team to a high standard, celebrating successes, taking personal responsibility for failures—these are basic principles of "we before me." Taking personal responsibility means accepting both the good and bad results of your actions, then moving on and being better tomorrow than you are today.

My parents had moved to Mississippi from Jacksonville, Florida, when I was three. In 1967, the year we arrived, the nation was beginning to experience racial turmoil similar to what we see today. The Mississippi Burning murders occurred only a few months before I was born, but racial tension in Mississippi was still very palpable in 1967. The Vietnam War was escalating, with troop levels reaching nearly 500,000 by the end of the year. The anti-war movement had not reached Mississippi and barely would (then as now, it is one of the most pro-military states in the nation).

My parents were products of their place (the Deep South) and time (the 1940s and beyond). So they had their biases, but even so, their Christian faith endowed them with a strong belief that all of God's children have equal value, and they made sure their children believed that, too. When I started first grade in Mississippi, mine was the first class (the future high school class of 1982) to go all twelve years in a desegregated school system. Mississippi had sued to preserve its segregated school system, lost the court battle, and in the 1970–71 school year integrated its public schools for the first time. Up to that point in my life, my church and rural community had been my whole world—and that world was almost completely white.

I remember going to the doctor's office as a little boy and seeing two separate waiting rooms, but that was nearly my only experience with negative attitudes toward black people at the time. I recall my mom telling me as I left for my first day of school there would be people different from me there. She made a point to tell me that although they might have different-colored skin than I did, God loved them equally as much. In my later years of elementary school, she and Dad intentionally interacted with an elderly black couple, Asa and Cynthia Evans, who owned a small cotton farm. My parents did this because they enjoyed their company, but also because they wanted their children to see that people who looked different than us were really the same.

As I think back on it now, the significance of Asa and Cynthia Evans farming cotton on their own land still encourages and inspires me to believe in the power of progress. I can still see their ancient clapboard house in my mind's eye. Like something from the movie *Forrest Gump*, it had a full front porch containing two well-weathered rocking chairs. On one of my parent's visits, I somehow got away from everyone, hopped up on Brother Asa's tractor, and fired it up. That created a commotion, and several of the elderly black women on the front porch made a big deal out of it. There was a lot of "Lord help us!" and "Save that child!" as the tractor bucked and rolled with me sitting in the driver's seat.

Sometimes Dad would take me with him on his regular visits to the Evanses' farm, and we'd just sit on Brother Asa's front porch and have coffee. Some today might attribute Dad's interest in that precious couple to some kind of white guilt, but nothing could be further from the truth. White guilt patronizes and condescends; my dad was genuinely concerned about Asa and his eternal soul, and told me that he wanted him to know Jesus, too. He knew that genuine love was the only way to build that bridge. Dad hoped to teach me to love Brother Asa as well. He succeeded.

My parents' faith contained another nugget that formed the basis of their "we before me" approach to life: Dad believed each person is uniquely created with a mission from God. That meant that failing to fully step into the vision He has for each life is tragic—and for me, it was totally unacceptable. Even getting a C in school was worthy of a spanking. Dad firmly believed that we are best served as a whole when each person "does his fair share" and lives out his intended purpose.

This assumption, coupled with the Parable of the Talents, provided the philosophical fuel for my parents' drive to make us the best we could be. That parable is a stewardship story. It teaches that each individual is granted talents and abilities, and that each is responsible for maximizing those gifts for the betterment of the whole. As the whole is made better, the Creator is gratified to see the gifts given being used to benefit all.

Despite my father's deep faith, we went to church only in spurts in my early years—attending faithfully for a while and then being absent for a stretch of time. I would later learn that was because Dad had felt an inward pull to preach and was fighting it—not unlike Jonah running from God's instruction to preach to the people of Nineveh. His resistance complicated his spiritual life for several years. Losing an arm and the ensuing financial crisis sufficiently drew his attention toward getting us back in church for a while. Hard times have a way of doing that.

Before I was born, my father served in the United States Air Force as a nuclear weapons technician stationed at Hahn, Germany, and was assigned to a nuclear response team from late 1958 to 1961. It was the height of the Cold War, so each day the pilot would fire up the jet, the crew chief would run his diagnostics, and Dad would reach into the nuclear device and flip the switch arming the nuclear bomb—and then disarm it. As Dad likes to say, "Then we would just sit around and wait for the war to start." Thank God, it never did.

Dad also served as the technician for conventional bombs including napalm, a petroleum-based explosive. One day, he somehow got napalm in his eye, requiring a visit to sick call. There, the provider noticed a slight deformity in Dad's forearm—the one he daily inserted into the nuclear device—and took an X-ray of it.

Some weeks later, Dad dropped by the medical unit and asked about his X-rays. The doctor was stunned nobody had called him, and immediately arranged for Dad to get to the regional medical center for a day's worth of tests. When the workup was complete, an Air Force physician told Dad he would need surgery and that he could no longer serve as a weapons technician. The Air Force offered him a cook's position or a medical discharge, but never told him why he needed surgery. Dad agreed to the surgery but didn't want to be a cook. When he chose the discharge, the Air Force sent him home with neither the operation nor an explanation. That's how he wound up working in a paper mill.

Nine years, a wife, three children, and a move to Mississippi later, a friend of my dad's who was a physician bought a new X-ray machine. Dad, believing he had some unique deformity but still not knowing exactly what it was, offered to have him test the machine on his arm. The result: Dad had osteosarcoma—bone cancer. A surgeon removed Dad's right arm from just above the elbow nearly two decades before President George H. W. Bush signed the Americans with Disabilities Act.

Such an event now would incentivize an employer to find a way to accommodate someone like my father in some way, perhaps by moving him to a supervisory position at a comparable salary. Instead, when Dad lost the biggest part of his dominant arm, the managers of the plant where he was working said, "You're half a man now. We're going to pay you half a salary." And they did.

That kind of double whammy has plunged many people into despair and substance abuse, and still others into bitterness toward God. But that is not how my father responded.

Despite the drastic cut in pay, Dad refused both government assistance and private charity. Instead, he took on additional jobs outside of work hours to close our family's new financial gap. With one arm, he painted and reroofed houses. If you'll spend a moment or two imagining trying to do those things with only one arm, you'll start to get a feel for the raw grit and determination this required. Painting houses with one hand is monumentally difficult, but not impossible.

But how would a one-armed man reshingle a house in the days before pneumatic nail guns were invented? Back then, you'd use one hand to hold the nail in place while the other swung the hammer. Dad solved this problem by laying aside his hammer, taking a roofing nail in his bare hand, and violently slamming it into the roof decking to get it started. Then he'd pick up his hammer and drive it the rest of the way in—repeating this process thousands of times until the job was done.

He also made outdoor furniture to sell, including picnic tables, benches, and Adirondack chairs. From the very beginning, I was his helper in those projects. The extra set of hands made a big difference. From that point forward, he would often refer to me in the presence of others as his "right-hand man" or simply "my right arm." It meant a lot to me as a boy to have the man I admired so much call me his right arm. I also proudly served as his designated shoe-tier.

Still, even with the odd jobs, things were hard financially. Eventually, my mother took a job when my baby brother went to school. At the time, I never really understood why potato soup was on the menu so often or why my mother inexplicably chose the neck on those special occasions when we had chicken. Dad and I got the breasts, and my sister and Rick got the legs and thighs, leaving Mom with the wings and the neck. I now know it wasn't preference that drove that choice; it was sacrificial love.

Resilience and responsibility characterized my father's life back then, and still do. However, there is a third virtue that he routinely modeled: selfless service to others. I view this trait as wholly admirable now, but as a teen, I frequently found it annoying. Because I was Dad's "right hand," I had to go along on his frequent trips of service. I vividly recall being rousted out of bed early one frigid January morning when school had been canceled because of a freak ice storm. My mother said that a neighbor who was sick in bed was out of firewood, and a wood stove was the only source of heat in that house—so Dad volunteered to cut and deliver some wood to the family. Obviously, if he was doing it, his right hand was going, too—and that meant me. I recall grumbling to him about it at the time. After all, the neighbor had two good arms and could have cut firewood long before the cold weather arrived, but my disabled father was heading out into the ice and cold to cut and carry firewood for their family. My dad's response was, "It doesn't matter, son. They need help. We're helping them."

My dad also modeled another great virtue: forgiveness. Despite having lost his arm because of a huge mistake made by the Air Force, and despite the lifelong hardship that created for him and us, I have never once heard him utter a negative comment about his service, the Air Force, or the country he served. He knew that blame and accusation would do nothing to change his circumstances, but it would change how he treated others—and most importantly, his expectations of how people should treat him. Dad would have no part in that.

I'm also grateful my parents taught us the value of work. They didn't just model it; they required it. When I wanted to play baseball,

Dad had me mow lawns to pay for the necessary equipment. At age ten, I took out a loan at the local Otasco Hardware Store for a mower, mowed neighbors' yards, and paid two dollars a week back to the store. At twelve, I took my first official paying job: Mike Russel owned a large pig barn a few miles away from our home. I'd ride my bike there each day after school, put on a full-body, water-proof slicker suit and rubber boots, and then hose out the concrete floors of the massive barn where the pigs were housed. All the waste had to be sprayed out into a catch pond. The smell was robust! After returning home from the job one day, my mom quipped, "Son, I know for certain that you're going somewhere in life, because from where you're starting, there's nowhere to go but up."

I once heard leadership guru John Maxwell say that his father defined "success" as living your life in such a way that those who know you best respect you most. There is a rich vein of gold to mine in that thought. The opposite is often the case for many of us. It's relatively easy to gain the respect of casual acquaintances who only see us when we're on our best behavior, but those who live with us every day see who we really are and what we're truly made of. By the above definition, my father, the one-armed laborer from rural Mississippi, is one of the most successful men I've ever known.

He wasn't perfect. No one is. But I witnessed greatness personified every day I was living under his roof. He simply refused to quit or be defeated by circumstances. And he never stopped serving others. It was always "we before me" for both him and Mom. As I write these words, he is in his early eighties and just recently retired from pastoring a church. He simply won't stop serving.

A few years ago, Dad wrote an autobiography titled *The Elusive Pea*—a humorous reference to the invariable struggle of a one-armed man chasing down that last green pea on the plate. It's a pretty good metaphor for a life that has beautifully displayed the virtue of deter-mined selflessness.

■ ■ ■

The opposite of "we before me" is "every man for himself." Any family, organization, community, or society that adopts that as its predominant ethic will quickly devolve into something hellish and dysfunctional that simply cannot prosper for long. That reality reminds me of an illustration I heard many years ago.

A gravely ill man has a dream in which a man in white, presum-ably an angel, transports him to a hallway lined with doors. He is led to one particular door, which is then opened. Inside, the man sees a long banquet table lavishly heaped with the most amazing foods of every sort, and people seated along each side. Each person has a very long-handled spoon or fork attached to each arm. The end of each utensil extends at least a foot beyond each hand. This means the banquet attendees cannot get the food to their mouths.

Looking closer still, the man sees that these individuals are emaci-ated and sickly. They are clearly starving to death with delicious-looking food piled high directly in front of them. The people at the table frantically stab and scoop at the food in a pitiful effort to get a morsel to their mouths, all in vain.

Appalled by what he has seen, the man turns to the person in white and asks, "What is this place?" The answer is horrifying: "You have seen Hell."

He is then led down the hallway to the next door. He enters and sees an identical banquet heaped with food. This table also is lined with people with the same long utensils bound to their arms, yet they seem well-fed and healthy. They are talking, laughing, and generally enjoying themselves. As he watches, he notices each person periodically dipping a spoon or fork into some of the food and serving one of the people sitting on the other side of the table. The figure in white looks at the man and says, "Now you have seen Heaven."

The difference between heaven and hell on earth is often not the external circumstances, but rather the hearts of the people in the midst of those circumstances. I've watched people in some of the grimmest situations imaginable finding joy and satisfaction because all involved embraced the "we before me" power of determined selflessness.

This virtue also works at much larger scales, including with entire nations.

■ ■ ■

I'm deeply proud to be an American. That pride is rooted in what I know of history. It is rooted in the sacrifices Americans have made over the last two centuries to build what some of the first settlers hoped would be "a shining city on a hill"—a beacon of freedom and hope for the whole world. And such it has been. Whenever there has been suffering or injustice in the world, we've been quick to offer aid and to defend the helpless.

Yet, many young people today have been taught a version of U.S. history that goes far beyond an honest "warts and all" telling of America's story—now they're hearing a "warts-only" version. Over the last forty years, countless high schools and colleges have made Howard Zinn's hypercritical and distorted *A People's History of the United States* the centerpiece of a history curriculum that amounts to little more than Marxist, anti-American brainwashing. As a result, many young Americans are deeply familiar with every instance in which we've failed to live up to the lofty ideals of our founding documents, but they know absolutely nothing of the myriad ways America has been a uniquely powerful source of good in the world.

Zinn's ideological DNA permeated the *New York Times*' twisted "1619 Project" that animated and (mis)informed so much of the social turbulence of the summer of 2020. Across the nation, statues of American founders and icons of Western civilization were toppled, defaced, or quietly removed. Throughout that time, I heard many genuinely bewildered people wondering out loud where all these young Americans who despise America came from. The answer is: We produced them. We've been incubating them in our schools, media, and popular culture for decades. They've been assured all their lives by teachers, pop stars, and activists posing as journalists that this flawed but extraordinary miracle of a place called America is truly monstrous.

Yet, for those of us who have been around awhile, these current events have a very familiar look and feel. That's because America hatched an earlier crop of Zinn disciples roughly ten years ago that manifested as the "Occupy" movement. The Marxist agenda then was the same as now: the downfall of capitalism, environmentalism as the official state religion, and the enshrinement of identity politics and "intersectionality" as the funhouse mirror through which all reality must be viewed.

There were prophetic voices trying to warn us forty years ago. Professor Allan Bloom's 1987 book, *The Closing of the American Mind: How Higher Education Has Failed Democracy and Impoverished the Souls of Today's Students*, foretold the events of the summer of 2020 with chilling accuracy. None of us who read it are remotely surprised that people are tearing down the statues of abolitionists, emancipators, and Spanish explorers today.

Robert Bork called it, too. In 1996, he wrote *Slouching Toward Gomorrah*, diagnosing the disease that now ravages the culture.

Radical individualism, radical egalitarianism, omnipresent
and omni-incompetent government, the politicization of
the culture, and the battle for advantages through politics
shatter a society into fragments of isolated individuals and
angry groups.[1]

Western culture, rooted deeply in Christian tradition, is the enemy
of those miseducated by Zinn and his evangelists. We have the
defaced, desecrated, and toppled statues of numerous "dead white
men" to prove it.

All of this grieves me because I know better. I've seen better. I've
walked among the seemingly endless rows of crosses and stars of
David on the beach at Normandy, where roughly nine thousand
Americans died in forty-eight hours during World War II. I've read
their stories. I've known their names. They and the families they left
behind gave all to free the world of tyranny.

Most conquering nations keep the land they've conquered as part
of the spoils of war. That's how empires are built. But not America.
All we've ever asked of our defeated foes is to be given a place to bury
our dead. What country in history has vanquished its enemy and then
spent billions to help them rebuild? We did that with the Marshall
Plan after World War II and in numerous other instances. The skeptics
and cynics in 2002 said we went to war in Iraq for oil. History has
rendered its verdict on that theory: It was a lie.

The Marxists like to pretend otherwise, but America was never
a colonial power like the Old-World nations of Europe. We could have
been, but it just wasn't in our collective DNA to build a globe-spanning
empire. Still, we've spent untold fortunes and spilled an ocean of
American blood to help other people become free. Many fail to recognize that the United States fought a war with itself to free men from
slavery. That is who we are. That is our legacy.

As you might suspect, I truly believe in American exceptionalism. That, too, has become unfashionable in many places lately, as have lots of other true, good, and noble things. We have been a great country, and a key source of that greatness has been our historic ability as a people to put "we before me."

CHAPTER 3

The Golden Triangle of Freedom
The Relationship between Virtue, Faith, and Freedom

Only a virtuous people are capable of freedom.

—Benjamin Franklin

I'd waited a long time to see my first combat deployment after graduating from West Point and joining in the Army in 1986. When the moment finally came, once I had finished medical school and joined the Night Stalkers, it was significant.

In October 2002, Congress authorized President George W. Bush to launch a military attack against Iraq if he deemed it necessary. He ultimately did, with a rationale that included several factors—not the least of which was that U.S. intelligence suspected Saddam Hussein was developing and stockpiling chemical and biological weapons, violating both international law and the ceasefire agreement forged after Operation Desert Storm in 1991. It was well known that Hussein's regime had previously deployed chemical weapons in the long, appallingly bloody war between Iraq and Iran, so finding and securing them was a high priority. Not surprisingly, the task would largely fall to America's special operations units.

The Iraq War officially began on March 20, 2003, when joint forces from the United States, United Kingdom, and other coalition partners unleashed a massive bombing that some Pentagon officials famously described as a "shock and awe" campaign. What most history books don't reveal is that some secretive, dangerous, special operations missions were executed inside Iraq two or three days before that full-scale launch. The Night Stalkers were assigned a major portion of the pre-launch missions. Our helicopters fired the first actual shots of the Gulf War, and my first combat mission soon followed.

Our target was a suspected biological weapons facility deep inside Iraq. As the medical officer assigned to that mission, that meant an extra level of preparation on my part. I not only needed to be equipped to treat injuries from chemical weapons, but from all sorts of injuries, while suited up from head to toe in chemical protective gear myself. Navy SEALs would assault and clear the target while a specialized WMD inspection team would search the target for the "smoking gun"—evidence that Hussein indeed had biological or chemical weapons or, at minimum, the active intent to create them. A flight medic and I would accompany the SEALs to that facility in a MH-47 helicopter designated as the primary casualty evacuation (CASEVAC) aircraft. Army Ranger units were tasked with providing additional security around the target.

As we approached the designated landing zone near the suspected facility, one of our other helicopters took enemy fire from the ground, and a door gunner was struck in the temple. A combat medic on board did the best he could using materials from the door gunner's own first-aid bag as the pilots diverted to a nearby airfield the Rangers had just secured. Another Ranger was struck in the chest during his team's insertion. Meanwhile, we continued with the SEALs in their assignment to secure the suspicious facility.

They found the complex abandoned but soaked in bleach. The Iraqis had either anticipated an early assault or had been tipped off. Of course, later many claimed there never were any banned weapons in Iraq and that their alleged presence served only as a pretense for the invasion, but I can't help but wonder why the surfaces in that facility had been wiped down with bleach so recently that the inspection team could still smell it strongly.

The medic sitting next to me on that mission was the senior medic for the 160th SOAR. Corey had greeted me soon after my arrival, while he was recovering from wounds sustained early in the invasion of Afghanistan, in one of the most storied and studied battles of that entire deployment.

Some may recall Operation Anaconda, in which U.S. Regular Forces joined Special Operations Forces in an attempt to find Osama Bin Laden among the caves of the Arma Mountains near Afghanistan's storied Khyber Pass. While aborting a plan to insert a Navy SEAL team on a mountain called Takur Ghar, Petty Officer First Class Neal Roberts fell from a helicopter and was captured by enemy forces. During the mission to rescue him, two Night Stalker aircraft were shot down on the mountain, where nineteen Army rangers, two Navy SEAL teams, and a handful of Night Stalkers battled an estimated 250 Taliban terrorists. Corey, who was trapped with them, cared for the wounded inside the perimeter during a seventeen-hour firefight. Over the course of the battle, he was shot seven times but continued to care for the other wounded until he passed out from blood loss. Eventually the survivors were rescued, and Corey was awarded the Silver Star. The incident proved to be the costliest of all the battles of

Operation Anaconda with seven Americans killed and twelve others wounded while adhering to the philosophy of "we before me."

It takes courage to go to war in the first place, but imagine the courage it takes to go back to the front lines only months after being shot seven times. Nevertheless, Corey sat comfortably and confidently next to me on my first combat mission.

Glen, the door gunner who was wounded on our mission, also exemplifies the courage of "we before me," both then and now. I met him the day before the mission, when one of our seasoned flight medics and I flew a rehearsal flight on Glen's aircraft. The flight medic introduced me to Glen and informed me that he had twice turned down opportunities to be promoted from sergeant to staff sergeant, which included a considerable pay raise, in order to stay on the aircraft. (Once a noncommissioned officer becomes a staff sergeant, they find themselves in a managerial position and not actually flying the missions.) Glen's love of flying and heart to serve went beyond recognition and pay. He knew the risks of staying on the aircraft. He placed his own life second to the mission; that takes courage. The injuries he sustained from the bullet were similar to that of a stroke patient. With courage, he pushed through recovery.

In the years since my time in combat, people often ask me to define courage. I start by telling them about Corey and Glen, and then say courage is not the absence of fear—it is simply valuing something more than yourself. That is the central meaning of "we before me."

A few days after that costly mission and frustrating outcome, the full-scale invasion of Iraq began, and coalition forces progressed rapidly toward Baghdad from the south. I soon found myself part of another special operations insertion that was right at, and perhaps just a little beyond, the "tip of the spear." And with it, both my personal virtue and my resourcefulness would be tested in an unusual and somewhat humorous way.

One of the first objectives of the coalition advance on the capital was to secure Baghdad International Airport—half of which is a typical civilian airport, and the other half a major base for the Iraqi Air Force and Republican Guard. In a major, highly coordinated assault, the U.S Army's 101st Airborne Division took and cleared the civilian side of the massive airport, while a contingent of SEALs and Rangers secured the military side.

The ground mission was assigned to a SEAL Team Six element and supported by Rangers. A Night Stalker flight medic and I inserted with them as their medical support team. Together we occupied an enormous hangar at the airport as our base for the mission. Our objective? To find and apprehend Saddam Hussein. Indeed, I had already participated in one SEAL mission aimed at capturing the Butcher of Baghdad, deep inside Iraqi territory. We had come up empty, but the aircraft I flew in was shot up so badly, it was unusable—"deadlined," in Army terms—for several weeks. The dictator was in the wind, and capturing him was a top coalition priority.

As soon as we were dropped at the airport, my first task was to find a vehicle to use as a makeshift ambulance. If one of our guys was wounded, I needed a way to transport him back to a field hospital in the forward staging area of the invasion. I began my search for a working vehicle near the remnants of the hangars there. I could hear the sounds of gunfire and explosions in the distance in several directions, as our guys were still in the process of pushing Hussein's forces out of Baghdad.

In fairly short order, I spotted a Nissan truck that would be perfect for the job. I approached it cautiously and on full alert. Although the Iraqis were in retreat, there was still the very real possibility that some snipers or other embedded forces had remained behind with orders to slow our advance. I was relieved to see that the truck was fully intact and unlocked, but with no keys present. That wasn't a problem, as one of the many skills I learned in the Army was how to hotwire vehicles.

I had just broken open the steering column and was about to pull the appropriate wires out when a large hand seized me roughly by the arm, yanked me out of the truck, and spun me around. I found myself face-to-face with very large beard, which was attached to an angry-looking man dressed in civilian clothes. I truly thought I was a dead man and that the next sound I heard would be a gunshot. Instead, I heard his voice, speaking to me in perfect New England-accented English. What a relief!

The bearded man was indeed on our side, a member of one our nation's intelligence agencies. He was quick to inform me that he had recently commandeered that truck for his own needs and that I would not be helping myself to it. I nodded, apologized, backed away, and dejectedly started looking around for plan B. He must have felt sorry for me because he called after me, "Hey, there's a brand-new blue Nissan Maxima down at the end of that runway. Still has the keys in the ignition."

That was great news, so I hustled in the direction he'd pointed and followed the airstrip. Sure enough, sitting like a pot of gold at the end of a concrete rainbow, there was a powder blue Maxima. I took a quick look around, hopped in, and twisted the key. Nothing. I popped the hood and quickly realized the battery was gone. For the second time in the last hour, my hopes had soared, only to be dashed.

I reluctantly started back toward our base of operations, imagining how I was going to tell the SEAL team commander that their shiny new flight surgeon with a Ranger tab and years of training as an infantry officer hadn't been able to secure an ambulance for evacuating his injured guys. I didn't like the way that imaginary conversation sounded in my head. (Anyone who's met a Navy SEAL understands that!) About that time, I was passing back by that Nissan pickup that the "agency guy" had claimed. The truck was still there but the beard was nowhere to be seen. I paused and thought for a moment, looked left and right, and took action. I popped the hood of the Nissan, quickly disconnected the battery, and surgically removed it.

Yes, against all the ethics and values of my upbringing, I brazenly stole that battery. (Complete the mission, right?) I then hurried back down the airstrip to the Maxima. It was a perfect fit!

The story doesn't end there, however. Several months later, I was in the post exchange near Baghdad. The PX, as it's called, is a bit like a mobile Dollar General store established for soldiers near a combat zone. As I stood in the checkout line holding a case of sodas, my stomach dropped as I watched the bearded agency guy walk in. I tried to disappear into the surrounding merchandise, to no avail. He recognized me and made a beeline for me, poked his finger into my chest and said, "Hey, buddy, did you take my battery that night you arrived in Baghdad?"

I took a deep breath and said, "I may be a thief, but I'm not a liar. Yes sir, I stole your battery." He stared into my eyes for a moment, then a smile spread across his face. "No worries, pal. To be honest, I had taken that battery out of the Maxima I sent you to get." Then he turned and headed into the store. *No wonder it was a perfect fit*, I thought.

This story it always draws a laugh when I tell it, but it illustrates a very important subject: Virtues such as honesty, self-reliance, self-control, courage, the concept of "leave no one behind," and a "failure is not an option" work ethic are not just for individuals, but for cultures and nations. In fact, as I'm about to show you, our hard-won, cherished freedoms are tightly linked to it.

■ ■ ■

"Do as you please. It's a free country."

How many times have you made or heard some variation of that statement in your life? Hundreds, perhaps thousands, I would guess. It's common because it's true. America is a "free country" because we are a free people. I think we take that for granted because we don't realize what a rare thing freedom has been in the long, tortured chronicle of this broken world. We don't grasp what a precious—actually, miraculous—thing we have inherited from previous generations of Americans.

A review of history reveals that oppression and servitude to a monarch or the state has been the default setting through the centuries. Sure, in many cultures, an elite class of individuals enjoyed some measure of liberty. Those fortunate enough to be born into the right lineage had basic freedoms such as the rights to choose a vocation, to hold private property, or to make the most of their talents and gifts. But for most people in most times, such freedoms were a fantasy. They still are in many parts of the world. Rigid caste systems and even slavery are still very present on Planet Earth—particularly those places least touched by Western values.

Many Americans who enjoy freedom and prosperity mistakenly think those things resulted from some random accident of history—that cosmic dice were rolled in the heavens and our nation won amazing levels of personal liberty and opportunity for bootstrap success. But our freedoms are no accident.

The gradual emergence of Western civilization, made possible by Christianity's sweep across Europe, sowed the seeds of something the world had never before seen—namely, a worldview and ethical framework that pointed toward social equality and freedom of opportunity for all people. Several recent books have made that case powerfully, including Rodney Stark's *The Victory of Reason: How Christianity Led to Freedom, Capitalism, and Western Success* and Tom Holland's *Dominion: How the Christian Revolution Remade the World.* This framework is incompatible with the concept of slavery, although it took centuries for that ancient and terrible institution to eventually collapse in the Western world. Again, only where these values undergird the culture is slavery considered abhorrent and illegal.

Writing about the thought of theologian and philosopher Reinhold Niebuhr, Francis Sempa noted:

> Western Civilization...is fragile. The belief that civilization and its institutions will survive without the support of the forces of order and religiously based virtuous restraint is a fatal delusion.[1]

This leads me to an important concept that allows us to understand the relationship between virtue and freedom.

Several years ago, the writing of Eric Metaxas first introduced me to the concept of the "Golden Triangle of Freedom,"[2] which he describes as the fact that "freedom requires virtue; virtue requires faith; and faith requires freedom."[3] Let's unpack that three-part proposition one part at a time.

Freedom Requires Virtue

Both history and common sense testify to the truth of that sentiment. Human flourishing requires order, peace, and broad respect for the rule of law. When individuals abandon virtue and do whatever their lowest impulses dictate, all these vital things disappear. Theft, violence, bribery, and every form of vice become the norm. Chaos results. And chaos invariably gives rise to dictatorships and other

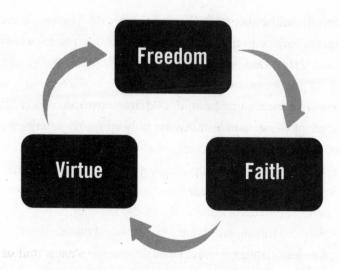

oppressive forms of authoritarian government as people become desperate for order at any price. That price is always personal liberty. Lenin, Hitler, Mussolini, Mao, Pol Pot, and a host of other brutal despots emerged in times of chaos, as people willingly traded their freedoms for the promise of restored order. A people who refuse to govern themselves will ultimately be governed by despots and dictators who provide at least some form of order—even if it is the order of the prison or the gulag. This is something the Founding Fathers of our nation understood very well. In a 1798 letter, John Adams, our second president, wrote:

> We have no government armed with power capable of contending with human passions unbridled by morality and religion. Avarice, ambition, revenge, or gallantry would break the strongest cords of our constitution as a whale goes through a net. Our Constitution was made only for a moral and religious people. It is wholly inadequate to the government of any other.[4]

Even rationalist skeptics affirmed this truth. Thomas Jefferson, who famously advocated in a letter for a "wall of separation between church and state," once wrote:

> No government can continue good but under the control of the people; and...their minds are to be informed by education what is right and what is wrong; to be encouraged in habits of virtue and to be deterred from those of vice....These are the inculcations necessary to render the people a sure basis for the structure and order of government.[5]

Yes, freedom requires virtue. In other words, to enjoy and sustain a form of government that permits maximum individual liberty requires a people and leaders who will govern their own worst impulses and bridle their darkest passions. As Os Guinness reminds us:

> [S]ustainable freedom depends on the character of the rulers and the ruled alike, and on the vital trust between them—both of which are far more than a matter of law. The Constitution, which is the foundational law of the land, should be supported and sustained by faith, character, and virtue of the entire citizenry....A republic grounded only in a consensus forged only of calculation and competing self-interests can never last.[6]

Scanning our current culture, it seems like a consensus of competing self-interests is all we have left. The Sexual Revolution of the late 1960s was about more than sex; it was about throwing off and throwing away—in the name of "freedom"—all of the mores, norms, and virtues that had made real freedom possible. It was about throwing away the very concept of right and wrong. The antiestablishment campus radicals of the 1960s and their disciples *are* the establishment today—with hands tightly on the levers of power in our educational, media, and bureaucratic institutions.

If you accept the proposition that freedom requires virtue—and for the sake of freedom in America, I hope you do—a question probably comes to mind: Why are some people generally virtuous and others not? That question brings us to the second side of that Golden Triangle.

Virtue Requires Faith

If you read the pamphlets, speeches, and private letters of the Founding Fathers, it becomes abundantly clear that they believed faith, or *religion*, in the vocabulary of their time, was vital to individual and community virtue. These men, on the whole, were far better versed in both history and philosophy than we tend to be today, yet over and over, we see them asserting that you can't have virtue without some universal moral code that transcends human opinion. Benjamin Franklin, no prude or saint himself, nevertheless wrote: "Men are so wicked as we now see them with Religion, what would they be without it?"[7]

They correctly observed that when you allow atheistic rationalism to shatter the constraints on human conduct, people and whole societies rapidly slide in a very dark direction. In fact, they witnessed from the other side of the Atlantic that very truth being validated in chaotic, bloody technicolor in the form of the French Revolution, which began just as the delegates of the thirteen colonies were ratifying our nation's Constitution.

Volumes have been written contrasting the American and French revolutions. Let it suffice to say that the differences are stark. America's revolution was anchored in her churches and informed by her preachers; the French revolutionaries shuttered and desecrated that nation's churches and executed the clergy. For example, in 1793, a mob of French revolutionaries looted the magnificent Notre Dame Cathedral, which at that time had stood in the heart of Paris for more than six hundred years. The mob pulled down dozens of statues of saints and publicly decapitated them. Once purged of Christian symbolism, Notre Dame and other cathedrals across France were, for a time, repurposed as "Temples of Reason."

The leading minds of France's new revolutionary religion declared it to be based on the ideals of reason, virtue, and liberty.[8] But by "reason," they meant rejecting the possibility of a holy, transcendent God, and by "liberty," they meant freeing themselves from the restrictive chains of the moral code. In other words, they were determined to violate the truths embedded in the Golden Triangle of Freedom. They believed they could have freedom without virtue and virtue without faith. They were wrong, and France descended into violent chaos until the people gladly traded it for the mirage of security provided by the authoritarian who would restore order—Napoleon Bonaparte.

Please don't misunderstand. The Founding Fathers did not believe that America had to be an overtly Christian nation in order to remain free, and neither do I. Yes, I am a Christian, so it is no surprise that I agree with Benjamin Franklin who, when asked to comment on Jesus Christ, said, "I think the system of morals and His religion as He left them to us, the best the world ever saw or is likely to see."[9] But I don't believe Christianity offers Americans the *only* moral code that can produce individual virtue. Rather, I am saying we must have a common moral framework, and we cannot trash the concept of absolute right and wrong, as so many in our "postmodern" culture have done, and long survive as a free people. We're already beginning to see the seeds of this bearing fruit in the form of riots and general lawlessness. Who can forget the Capitol Hill Autonomous Zone in Seattle, and the fires, rapes, and murders that took place while the police were kept out?

Virtue requires faith, just as freedom requires virtue. This brings us to the third side of the triangle.

Faith Requires Freedom

It is no accident that wherever dictatorships and totalitarian governments have arisen, religious freedom has been one of the first casualties. The Founders understood this, which is why freedom of religion is the very first among the five core freedoms enshrined in the First Amendment to the Constitution. It's also why the totalitarian impulses of the woke zealots and cancel-culture fanatics are focused so keenly on religion, but I will expound on that in a later chapter.

Let's look around the globe. For most of the twentieth century, the Soviet Union and its client states brutally crushed all forms of religious belief and expression. In our own day, we're seeing something very similar under the Chinese Communist Party (CCP) in mainland China. There, churches have been meeting underground for decades as Christians have suffered numerous waves of brutal persecution involving systematic imprisonment and torture. Where churches are found, the CCP removes their crosses and forces them to replace them with an image of the "Premiere Leader." Over the last twenty-five years, followers of the Falun Gong religious movement have been the focus of similar repression. Recently, reports of the plight of the Uyghurs, a predominantly Muslim people in northwestern China, have begun to leak out, including documentation of horrifying mass incarceration, torture, forced sterilization, and forced abortion.

These faiths tend to experience persecution because they represent a competitive threat to China's official state religion—the Communist

Party itself. And it's not just China; all oppressive governments and societies demand religious loyalty and a form of worship. This points us to the genius of the way America's Founders framed the First Amendment: "Congress shall make no law prohibiting the establishment of religion or prohibiting the free exercise thereof."

We generally tend to focus on the last part of that sentence, commonly known as the "free exercise" clause. And it's certainly vital that government authorities do not restrict or repress expressions of religious faith and worship (as the Soviets did and the CCP still does). However, the first part of that premise is equally important. The Founders had seen the bloodshed and suffering that result when a nation adopts an official state religion and forces allegiance to it. As we've seen, that is true even when the official state religion is atheism. The framers of the Constitution recognized that we can come to genuine faith only when we are at liberty to choose it without coercion by the state.

In other words, there is no faith without freedom. And there is no freedom without virtue, and no virtue without faith. This is the Golden Triangle of Freedom. Putting "we before me" means valuing not only one's own liberty, but liberty for us all.

■ ■ ■

I hope that a significant number of my fellow Americans will discover and embrace the validity of this trio of truths. Why? Because freedom is precious and fragile, and it is deceptively easy to surrender, little by little. More than fifty years ago, Ronald Reagan warned us:

Perhaps you and I have lived with this miracle too long to be properly appreciative. Freedom is a fragile thing and is never more than one generation away from extinction. It is not ours by inheritance; it must be fought for and defended constantly by each generation, for it comes only once to a people. Those who have known freedom and then lost it have never known it again.[10]

It is a timely warning today because we are increasingly a people who would rather be taken care of than be free. And Franklin warned, "They who can give up essential liberty to obtain a little temporary safety deserve neither liberty nor safety."

I am no conspiracy theorist. But there are some in America who fervently buy into the Marxist ideology. They need the chaos I mentioned before to allow authoritarianism to be accepted, so they plan chaos. Of course, in their model, they become the elites in charge. It begs the question: Is there a counter triangle—one of tyranny that serves as the opposite to the triangle of freedom? If there were, it might look something like this:

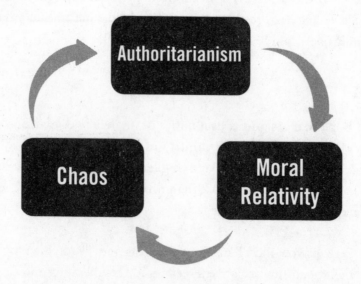

The chaos is necessary for a people to ask for a Bonaparte. When you have moral relativity, believe life is not precious, burn cities, or punch someone in the face for looking too Jewish, you have that chaos. Authoritarianism supports the moral relativity because with the centralized control of the media and the message, one can dictate what people can say and cancel them when they fail to conform.

If you're of a certain age, you will surely remember the great radio newsman and storyteller Paul Harvey. For six decades, beginning in the 1940s, Americans trusted the comforting, baritone voice of the man who became famous for telling us "the rest of the story."

What many of us who remember him mainly for his intriguing takes on historical figures or quirky news items about small-town America don't realize is that in the 1950s, Paul Harvey was one of the most powerful national media voices warning about the dangers of creeping socialism. In his 1952 book *Remember These Things*, Harvey wrote passionately about the relationship between virtue and freedom—particularly the virtue of self-reliance. One passage in particular bears quoting at length:

> We have been lured into a trap.
>
> In the past two decades in the United States, a benefi-cent government has sold us a substitute for freedom. It is called security.
>
> At the polls, the people thought that was what they wanted. Security. Suddenly the gamble was taken out of job-seeking. Taxes took all the excess profits—the bonus of business. We were promised that the government will take care of us if we get ill or get old and that we shall never earn less than forty cents an hour no matter what.
>
> Thus, we have lost the good sense and moral integrity that set man apart [from the animals]...we are all trying

to get something for nothing. If the old pioneering fire has died out of us, if we will hang onto new deals, fair deals and raw deals at the sacrifice of our I-deals, then we deserve to be trapped by our own clutching fingers because we are animals, nothing more.

History, for six thousand years, is the record of free people made slaves trying to get the free lunch out of the bottle. Lincoln said, "Let not him who is houseless pull down the house of another, but let him work diligently and build one for himself."[11] ... We said we no longer wanted "opportunity." We wanted "security." And they gave us chains. And we were secure.[12]

Harvey was alarmed by the trends he saw in place nearly seventy years ago. He saw growing numbers of people willing to trade their freedom for false and illusory promises of security and "free stuff with other people's money." How much farther down that road have we traveled since then?

We cannot be both free and amoral. Libertines cannot preserve liberty—not for long, anyway. Virtue is essential to freedom, and therefore "we before me" is as well.

CHAPTER 4

Absolute Power Corrupts Absolutely

A Society without "We Before Me"

Many of the greatest tyrants on the records of history have begun their reigns in the fairest manner. But this unnatural power corrupts both the heart and the understanding.

—Edmund Burke

It was utterly surreal. I had seen his mustachioed image thousands of times in the news footage, but now I was face-to-face with the Butcher of Baghdad, Saddam Hussein. What's more, we were locked together in a small room, along with my "terp" (interpreter), and an intelligence officer who happened to be asleep. It would just be the four of us all night long. Hussein was gesturing for me to take his blood pressure like I was the hired help.

These were the opening few moments of one of the strangest and most remarkable nights of my life. Perhaps I should back up and explain how I landed in this situation.

In the collective American memory, there was only one justification presented for the 2003 invasion of Iraq: the suspected presence of weapons of mass destruction. In reality, the case for action was a braided rope of numerous cords.

One strand was the objective of finding and capturing known international terrorists operating within Iraq. History reveals that one of those terrorist cells would eventually come to call itself "Al Qaeda" in Iraq and would later change its name to "ISIL" or "ISIS." Another goal was to gather as much intelligence as possible about the international web of terrorist networks which, as 9/11 revealed, had come to span the globe. A third group of stated objectives involved ending Saddam Hussein's regime, thereby enabling the world to end economic sanctions on the country and begin delivering aid to displaced, oppressed, and suffering people in the region. This would hopefully put Iraq's vast oil wealth into the service of helping all Iraqis rather than just the dictator's family and cronies.

Nevertheless, the objective of identifying, securing, and disposing of Iraq's WMDs was clearly the most spectacular piece of that broad case, generating the most headlines and recognition. This is probably why the failure to find a WMD smoking gun would later be the reason both opponents of the invasion and critics of President George W. Bush would focus on it.

I mentioned in the previous chapter how one of our very first missions inside Iraq, days before the full-scale invasion, was focused on capturing and investigating a suspected biological or chemical weapons site, and that it had been freshly washed with bleach when we arrived. It is also telling that on our initial special operation missions, we all had to be fully dressed out in our Level 4 MOPP gear. MOPP (Mission Oriented Protective Posture) requires one to be covered head to toe in something like a hazmat suit—which are heavy, cumbersome, and claustrophobic under the best of conditions. Combat operations in an Iraqi desert are *not* the best of conditions.

Our leaders weren't jerking us around by making us wear that gear. Everyone, top to bottom, genuinely anticipated that we might be attacked with mustard gas or nerve agents, and with good reason. There was overwhelming evidence that Hussein had used such weapons, both in Iraq's eight-year war with Iran and against the Kurdish minority within his own country—killing five thousand of them in a single day in 1988, and untold numbers more as the years went by from the lingering effects of the chemicals.[1]

Some of the confusion on the issue of WMD in Iraq stems from misperceptions about what the term "weapons of mass destruction" means. Many think it almost exclusively means conventional *nuclear* weapons—but it is broader than that, encompassing nuclear, radio-active, chemical, and biological weapons. There was no real doubt that Hussein developed, possessed, and deployed to terrible effect at least some of these types of weapons in the 1980s and 1990s. The only unanswered question was whether he had complied with the cease-fire terms of the first Gulf War—triggered by his invasion of Kuwait—which required Iraq to dispose of all banned weapons. Ten years later, there were many reasons to suspect that he had failed to fully comply with that order, or in the interim had secretly restarted his banned-weapons programs.

As it happened, when I was based in Baghdad International Airport, I saw with my own eyes a Boeing 727 airliner painted with the corporate insignia of Iraq's national airline in order to look like a passenger jet, but with all the seats removed and reinforced freight flooring installed. This was one in a small fleet of similarly modified aircraft, including at least one 747, that were rumored to have flown Hussein's stores of banned weapons into Syria just before Baghdad fell to coalition forces.

Yet Hussein's list of atrocities extends far beyond his use of banned weapons. He rose to power in the late 1970s through ruth-lessness and cruelty, and maintained power the same way. Dissent was crushed and dissenters were often tortured and killed in front of their families in order to perpetuate an atmosphere of fear and sub-mission. In 2006, ABC News reported:

> The exact number of deaths attributable to Saddam
> Hussein may never be known, but estimates range as high
> as half a million. There is evidence of more than 250 mass
> graves dating to his rule....The most notorious is his geno-
> cidal campaign against the Kurds in the north.[2]

Many more mass graves have been located since that report was written. According to the UN, between three thousand and four thousand Kurdish villages were destroyed in Hussein's genocidal campaigns against them.[3] In at least one case, and probably many, Iraqi Army soldiers entered a village and rounded up every male over the age of five. Those people were never seen again, but years later, mass graves discovered nearby suggest they were all executed.[4]

When the tyrant wasn't committing mass murder in the north of the country, he was destroying the culture and environment of the Marsh Arabs of the south. The vast delta formed where the legendary Tigris and Euphrates Rivers empty into the Persian Gulf and was at one time considered one of the most important wetlands on Earth. It was also home to a special culture of Shiite Muslim Arabs who had been living there for centuries. Hussein, a member of a Sunni sect of Islam that, at least in Iraq, was significantly outnumbered by the Shia, had big plans for their homeland and also viewed them as a potential threat. So, he instituted a massive government drainage plan while forcing the Marsh Arabs off the land. The drainage project became an environmental disaster of gigantic proportions. Before Hussein targeted the area, roughly a quarter of a million people called it home. Today, an estimated forty thousand people remain in the area, since 90 percent of it is uninhabitable.[5] Human Rights Watch labeled the campaign a crime against humanity.[6] As recently as 2019, human rights researchers were finding mass graves in southern Iraq, many of them filled predominantly with women, children, and infants.[7]

Sadly, the catastrophe of the southern marshes would not be the only human and environmental disaster directly attributable to Hussein. As previously mentioned, he triggered the first Gulf War when he invaded Kuwait in August 1990. As he was being pushed back out by the coalition forces of Operation Desert Storm, Hussein ordered Kuwait's vast oil fields set ablaze and the oil delivery pipelines near the Persian Gulf ruptured.

More than seven hundred wells were blown apart and ignited. It took more than ten months to extinguish all the blazes, which converted more than a billion barrels of oil into black smoke and created hundreds of oil lakes filled with hundreds of millions of barrels' worth of crude oil.[8] Much of the region became a sunless, toxic hellscape. Roughly ten million barrels of oil spilled into the Gulf, significantly damaging the coastal ecosystems.[9]

Clearly, Hussein earned the moniker the "Butcher of Baghdad" the old-fashioned way. One writer summed it up by saying:

> Saddam Hussein was unquestionably one of the most brutal dictators of the twentieth century. History cannot even begin to record the full scale of his atrocities and the effect they had on those affected and the families of those affected.[10]

All of the above is just a sliver of the evil perpetrated by Saddam Hussein throughout his years in power, and I haven't even touched on the horrors and atrocities perpetrated by his two sons, Uday and Qusay. All three represent a vivid "Exhibit A" for the maxim that power corrupts, and absolute power corrupts absolutely. I have recounted some of these crimes here only to help you understand why removing him from power was a significant and frequently overlooked aspect of the mission that would constitute the largest U.S. special operations action since the Vietnam War, and ultimately bring me face-to-face with the "Ace of Spades."

■ ■ ■

Operation Iraqi Freedom officially began on March 20, 2003, and by the first week of April, I was setting up shop in that hangar at Baghdad International Airport. By May 1, the bulk of the combat operations were over, but the Hussein administration, along with a significant number of terrorist leaders, had been run to ground—in some cases, literally. The first gulf war had left Hussein in office as dictator of Iraq. The second one couldn't make that same mistake.

The task of locating and apprehending the rats fleeing the sinking ship fell to America's special operators with the help of the intelligence services, operating under a banner called Taskforce 121 or TF-121. I became one of a handful of doctors assigned to work for its energetic and resourceful leader, Admiral Bill McCraven, a stellar "we before me" leader.

A list of fifty-two high-value targets (HVTs) was compiled. That number reminded some clever person of a deck of cards, so the name of each card in a standard deck was assigned to a specific fugitive. The higher the value of the target, the higher the card name assigned. The face cards in this deck were many of Hussein's generals and top government officials. The King of Spades was Hussein's first cousin and top official in the Iraqi government, Ali Hasan al-Majid, widely known as "Chemical Ali" for his role in ordering the use of chemical weapons against civilians.

The Ace of Diamonds was Hussein's right-hand man, presidential secretary Abid Hamid Mahmud al-Tikriti. Uday and Qusay Hussein were the Aces of Hearts and Clubs, respectively. The biggest HVT of all—Saddam Hussein—was the Ace of Spades.

In the months after the end of combat operations, that deck stack got progressively shorter as many of the targets on the list were apprehended by special forces units. In June, a Delta Force team, accompanied by a British Special Air Service (SAS) team and an array of other support units, captured the Ace of Diamonds. Uday and Qusay were killed in a firefight in July when, acting on an informant's tip, special forces units surrounded a house in Mosul where they had been hiding.

Months passed, however, without any breakthrough on the capture of the Ace of Spades. In that interim, I enjoyed a couple of months at home as I rotated out of the active zone in accordance with our special operations unit's rotation policy. Upon my return to Iraq, the hunt for Saddam remained a top priority for TF-121. Finally, nearly nine months after the launch of Operation Iraqi Freedom, a breakthrough came.

I recount in detail the hunt for and capture of Hussein in my book, *A Night with Saddam*. Here, I will just say that I came perilously close to missing my date with destiny. Hussein's surprise capture—he was literally hiding in a hole in the ground nine miles outside his hometown—occurred just a day before I was scheduled to rotate back home again. The assignment that put me face-to-face with him throughout his first night in captivity came purely by chance. I simply happened to be standing in the right place at the right time.

I don't believe in coincidences. In fact, on the day before Hussein was captured, my father and many of his pastor friends back in Mississippi had embarked on a day of fasting and prayer for me and for the mission. To my dad's way of thinking, the sooner Hussein was captured, the sooner I could get safely home to my family—but my mother was specifically praying that I would be given the opportunity to participate in his apprehension at some level before I returned home. Coincidence? You can't convince me of that.

■ ■ ■

There is an eight-hour time difference between Iraq and Mississippi. So, at midnight on December 12, 2003, just a few hours after the folks back home finished their day of fasting and prayer, U.S. intelligence personnel in Iraq received a tip concerning the possible whereabouts of Saddam Hussein. A few hours after that, I found myself fully dressed for action and on a helicopter carrying special operators north toward Tikrit, Hussein's hometown and power base. I was the flight surgeon on this mission with the role of evacuating any casualties; standard practice was to land near the target and wait with the pilot, blades still turning, monitoring the radio chatter, and hoping we wouldn't be needed.

What we heard on our radios for the first hour or so sounded like a lot of frustration. A search of two farm sites had turned up nothing. Suddenly, the energy level of the chatter ramped way up.

"We've got Jackpot," a voice said.

The mission commander requested a repeat of that message.

"We've got Jackpot!" the excited voice said once more.

Then I heard a voice I recognized as Admiral McCraven's. Throughout scores of missions to apprehend the HVTs in our "most wanted" deck of cards, I had never once heard him speak on the radio. But here he was in the conversation, asking, "Do you mean *big* Jackpot?"

The reply came back, "Affirmative. We have big Jackpot."

Instantly, those of us on the blacked-out special operations CASEVAC helicopter were exchanging high-fives and slapping each other on the back. We were ecstatic.

Less than a few hours after receiving the tip, the Ace of Spades was being pulled out of his underground "spider hole." The pictures that later emerged show a haggard, disheveled, bearded man squinting in bewilderment at the bright lights pointed at him. The special operations guys who found him said Hussein's words (in English) as he surrendered himself were, "My name is Saddam Hussein. I am the president of Iraq and I want to negotiate." One of our guys instantly replied, "Regards from President Bush." Hussein was restrained, hooded, and loaded into a small helicopter for transfer to a secure location.

We headed back to base, and I assumed that would be the end of it for me. After all, I was scheduled to fly home the next day. But I was so amped up from the excitement, I took the short, familiar walk over to the interrogation facility to which Hussein had been delivered. His capture was a momentous event with historic implications, and I simply wanted to be as close as possible to whatever happened next. Soon, I found myself sitting outside the door of the room in which he was being held.

There was no interrogation going on behind that door. In fact, the intelligence guys wanted Hussein to rest overnight before beginning their questioning in the morning. Around midnight, one of the senior intelligence officers in the hallway recognized me and said the admiral wanted a medical officer with the prisoner at all times. After months of expending precious blood and treasure in the quest to capture the dictator, the last thing anyone wanted was for something to happen to him on his first night in U.S. custody—anything from a heart attack due to the stress of capture, to some sort of self-inflicted attempt at martyrdom.

That's how I found myself tasked with babysitting the Butcher of Baghdad with the assistance of an interpreter. I figured he'd be sleeping, so I grabbed a nearby copy of *Stars and Stripes*, took a deep breath, and headed through the door.

When I entered, Hussein was lying under a blanket on a cot on the opposite side of the room. A colleague of mine had examined him when he first arrived and had obviously gotten him shaved and cleaned up. He looked nothing like the grimy hermit that had been extracted from a hole in the ground a few hours earlier. The room was fully illuminated, so he had his hand over his eyes. I assumed he was asleep, but when the interpreter and I exchanged a few words, Hussein suddenly bolted upright in bed. It was rather startling, to say the least. Spotting the stethoscope hanging around my neck, he demanded in Arabic that I take his blood pressure and gestured toward his arm. I did so, because looking after his health was precisely what I had been put in that room to do. Yet his manner made it clear that he was accustomed to being waited on and attended to, and that he thought I was there to serve him.

Afterward, he laid down again for a bit, then sat up again. This time his manner was less imperial, and he initiated a conversation. Through the interpreter, he mentioned that when he was young, he'd considered becoming a doctor. Suddenly, the man who had ruled Iraq with an iron fist and been responsible for the deaths of hundreds of thousands of innocents was feeling chatty. In fact, he didn't stop talking for the next five hours. I pulled out a pen and started using my newspaper as a notepad.

As I've said, you can find the details of that long conversation in *A Night with Saddam*. I want to highlight one moment here because it speaks directly to the theme of this chapter and to the larger theme of "we before me."

Somewhere in the wee hours of the morning, I asked Hussein why he had invaded Kuwait ten years earlier, knowing that his invasion and subsequent expulsion by American and coalition forces had sown the seeds that ultimately led to his downfall and to the very conversation we were having that night. I'll never forget his surprising response.

He held out his hand and pointed to his palm, then traced the line that begins as one and forks into two. Iraqis are raised to view the palm as a "map" of their homeland, and those two lines represent Iraq's most iconic and distinguishing topographical features, the Tigris and Euphrates rivers. Both find their headwaters in the mountains of eastern Turkey, diverge in northern Syria, and run roughly parallel through the length of Iraq, until seemingly reconnecting once more as they empty into the Persian Gulf. I knew that those rivers had nurtured life and agriculture and empires for millennia, and that the land between them has long been known as the "cradle of civilization." I also knew well that the book of Genesis describes the Garden of Eden, and therefore the birthplace of mankind, as being near them.

Clearly, Hussein knew this as well. Pointing to those forked lines on his hand, he matter-of-factly stated that Iraq was the point of origin for all humanity. It was logical then, he explained, to view all the people of the world as Iraqi—including the people of Kuwait. And as the God-ordained ruler of Iraq, he therefore had the right to enter Kuwait and do with it as he pleased.

Think about that for a moment. By Hussein's twisted logic, he was the rightful ruler of every person on earth! I've read enough history to have encountered megalomania before. Hitler saw himself as the founder of a third German empire that would last for a thousand years. Pol Pot, a communist dictator in Cambodia, murdered more than two million of his own people, purging his nation of anyone who could threaten his rule. Few in history have ever had the nerve to calmly assert a right to rule the entire world, yet the man sitting before me had just done so. Perhaps I shouldn't have been surprised. In researching our target, I had read somewhere that he viewed himself as the reincarnation of Nebuchadnezzar II, the greatest king of the storied Babylonian Empire.

Hussein had wielded nearly unlimited power in Iraq for more than two decades, and it was clear to me that unchecked power had done terrible things to his mind and soul.

■ ■ ■

Spending an entire night listening to one of the twentieth century's most ruthless mass murderers talk about himself without the slightest hint of remorse or self-doubt was a jarring experience, perhaps even more so because it was the opposite of the leadership I'd seen modeled while growing up, in every way. I'd watched my father lead our family and churches with an approach that I now know has a name— "servant leadership." His attitude was sacrificial, unselfish, and put the needs of the whole unit ahead of his own; he lived a life of determined selflessness. That's the essence of "we before me." Without the dual constraints of a moral code and external accountability that checks our choices, we human beings are all capable of great evil. The Bible offers a compelling explanation for this: As humans, we're all inwardly broken and twisted versions of what God originally intended us to be. The Framers of the U.S. Constitution understood this well, and instituted a brilliant system of checks and balances to ensure we never vested too much power in one set of hands. Those same Founders also sought to constrain national government with the strong chains of constitutional limits on federal power.

Many of our most modern ideologies—secular humanism, for example—deny the basic facts of human nature. People who hold to

this belief system view humans as inherently good and born perfect—
or at least perfectible, if only the right elites are vested with suffi-
cient power. They fail time and again because you can't repeal
human nature; you can only guard against it. As Jonah Goldberg
reminds us:

> The story of civilization is, quite literally, the story of
> taming, directing, channeling, or holding at bay, human
> nature.... Civilizations—all of them—establish rules of one
> kind or another to direct or channel human nature toward
> productive ends. What counts as productive ends has
> evolved over time. For most of the last 10,000 years, pro-
> ductive ends were defined as "what is good for the rulers."
> Since the Enlightenment, the definition has improved. The
> modern ideologies of socialism, nationalism, and democ-
> racy all claim that the ends of a just society must be the
> betterment of "the people." But human nature being what
> it is, the elites of every society often find ways to benefit
> nonetheless. And definitions of "the people" often turn out
> to be quite selective.[11]

What's true at the macro level for whole societies is also true at
the micro level for businesses and even families. We ignore the realities
of human nature at our peril. That's what I took away from an all-
night conversation with Saddam Hussein, the Butcher of Baghdad.

CHAPTER 5

Until They Know How Much You Care

How "We Before Me" Can Empower Your Company

The first responsibility of a leader is to define reality.
The last is to say thank you. In between the two, the
leader must become a servant and a debtor.

—Max De Pree

After 9/11, it became clear that we were fighting a new kind of war against a new kind of enemy. Historically, wars were fought against national armies under centralized command, but the terrorist networks we now faced, embedded in places as diverse as Afghanistan, Iraq, and the Philippines, were loosely affiliated, semi-autonomous, and decentralized. Our entire military mindset—starting with our elite special forces—needed to be retooled on the fly.

Stanley McChrystal, commanding general of the Joint Special Operations Command (JSOC) was one of the key individuals tasked with engineering that sweeping change. In his 2015 book *Team of Teams: New Rules of Engagement for a Complex World*, McChrystal gives us a glimpse of that initial challenge:

The genesis of this story lies in the transformation of an elite military organization, the Joint Special Operations Task Force...in the midst of a war. We could compare ourselves during that transition to a professional football team changing from one offensive system to another in the second quarter of a critical game, but the reality was far more drastic. The Task Force's shift was actually more akin to that team's moving from playing football to basketball and finding that habits and preconceptions had to be discarded along with pads and cleats.[1]

If a corporate manager fails at leadership, the company may have a bad quarter. If battlefield commanders fail at leadership, more men return to their loved ones in flag-draped coffins, and the fates of entire nations may turn in a dark direction. I've discovered that many of the leadership principles that make America's special operators the finest and most formidable in the world translate seamlessly to organizations in the private sector. After leaving active military service in 2009, I founded a healthcare company. I knew that hospitals all over the nation often contracted the operation of their emergency rooms out to third parties. My goal was to create a world-class team that would meet that need, and did. Align MD, named with the intention of aligning physicians' and hospital executives' incentives to better serve patients, grew from $180,000 in annual revenue and one employee—me!—in year one to over $200 million in annual revenue and more than 1,000 full- and part-time providers and staff by year eight. We doubled in revenue every year as I applied the "we before me" leadership principles. These include:

1. There is power in an "elite" culture.
2. Leading well takes humility.

3. Leading requires love.
4. Leading requires integrity.
5. Leading means facilitating your people's best.
6. Leaders must be seen.

■ ■ ■

1. There Is Power in an "Elite" Culture

Your organization will have a culture one way or another—so you must take determined measures to ensure it's a good one. Think of an "elite" culture as you would athletes or special operations units. When members of a team come to believe they are a part of the best of the best, it becomes a self-fulfilling prophecy.

This is an incredibly powerful principle. We all desire to belong to something bigger than ourselves. We're hardwired for community. Like a double-edged sword, this psychological-spiritual force makes certain college football programs perennial contenders for national championships and also drives the toxic tribalism I mentioned earlier.

Some people gravitate toward groups that will speak to their higher nature, appeal to their desire for greatness, and challenge them to reach their full potential. Others find themselves in cultures that do just the opposite. Such groups appeal to low motives like greed and resentment. Rather than calling people to excellence, they're taught to make excuses, do the bare minimum, and tear down others who strive to do better.

The transformative power of group identity is extraordinary. The motto "Night Stalkers don't quit" was our identity as a unit. And when I joined, little by little, it became my identity, too. I experienced this on an even more profound level when I became a Christian. The Bible teaches that transformative experience actually imparts a new identity.

I was adopted into a new family, one in which God became my Father and my fellow believers my brothers and sisters. I soon learned that my group identity included a commitment to love, forgiveness, purity, generosity, and a host of other attributes and practices.

Understanding the universal need to belong is a vital tool in the kit of successful leaders. Wise leaders clearly define the group identity—the values, ethics, virtues, and distinctives—and then relentlessly infuse it into every aspect and process. In his great little book on leadership, Bob Boylan says the principal role of a leader is to "define what's important around here to all of us."[2]

By the time I reported to the commander of the 160th Special Operations Aviation Regiment, I had graduated from West Point with an economics degree, graduated from the Army's Ranger School, commanded in the famed 82nd Airborne Division, graduated in the top third of my medical school, and graduated from the top U.S. residency program in emergency medicine. And, as I saluted the commander to join this elite, "best of the best" special operations unit, I wondered in the back of my mind if I was good enough to be there.

How many people who come to work for your company wonder if they are good enough to be on your team? No one wants to play for the worst team in the NFL; they all want to be on a championship team. Every player on the Super Bowl-winning team is working overtime to stay on it. An elite culture is a very powerful thing.

I started Align MD from scratch and knew that creating the right culture would require developing leaders who saw themselves as the best of the best and still lucky to be on a team as good as ours. That's hard to do when a company is very young. So with only two accounts and about twenty-five employees, I started the Align MD Leadership Academy.

I told people that to stay on a team as special as ours, the leaders must live the motto of "we before me." Our leadership classes were top-rate and intended to be culture combat multipliers. I never required those receiving the costly development classes to commit to a term of service at Align MD. Some may say it's foolish to develop leaders who can leave your team and go elsewhere—but why would they ever want to go elsewhere if our company is the best?

At the very outset of an interview with a physician or physician leader hoping to join our company, we made it clear that we were a different kind of organization—and to join our team they had to be, too. It worked. John Maxwell often talks about the unique challenge of leading a volunteer-staffed organization, in that volunteers can leave at any point. Keeping emergency rooms staffed presents a related challenge: Emergency physicians are typically paid by the hour or by the volume of patients they see. Their "customers" are one-offs, meaning the physician doesn't have to maintain patient loyalty as those in a practice do. Furthermore, most hospitals in America have understaffed ERs, and therefore, ER docs tend to move around a lot. In fact, the turnover rate in a year for emergency physicians exceeds 20 percent in many places. Yet, at Align MD, our turnover was less than 4 percent.

Culture is only a means to an end, but it still must be a clear target on the wall if you want it to be healthy. To get to "we before me," every member of the company had to sign our culture statement, which I've provided in the notes section.[3]

If you want an elite culture, define what that looks like for your organization, ask everyone to commit to live by it, and expect them to do so. And if they don't, tell them to leave. Elite organizations never give participation trophies.

2. Leading Well Takes Humility

While serving in Afghanistan, I ran into a great friend from a former assignment to Fort Benning, Georgia. Bill was a Special Forces

Green Beret officer who had just gone through the battalion command selection board. The list had just been published when we met at a dusty airstrip in the remote Hindu Kush. While Bill and I had not seen each other in years, we followed each other's career and so, when I saw him, I was already aware he had not been selected to command a battalion. I expected to see frustration, maybe even anger, and certainly disappointment.

But when I brought it up, he said, "You know, Mark, at some point in life, the act of service should be reward enough." His response rang with maturity and wisdom and had a profound impact on me. I wrote his words down that night, and they have powered my approach to life, leadership, and service ever since.

Such an attitude can only rest on a foundation of humility. Most people equate leading with being served rather than with serving. They assume promotion brings only perks and privileges. Indeed, in some organizations that view reflects reality—but those organizations rarely thrive for long.

The most effective approach is found in the ancient wisdom of the Judeo-Christian Scriptures. As a medical professional, I find an account of a remarkable conversation between a controversial leader of that day and his core leadership team, recorded by a first-century doctor, to be especially meaningful. The leader's words are doubly weighty because he had just told his team he was about to be arrested and executed for offending the ruling powers. This prediction triggered a discussion among his executives about who should rise to fill the new vacancy. That discussion was escalating into an argument when the leader, overhearing them, interrupted and challenged their entire paradigm:

> "In this world the kings and great men lord it over their people.... But among you it will be different. Those who are

the greatest among you should take the lowest rank, and the leader should be like a servant." (Luke 22:25–26 NLT)

What a difference that made! The bickering status-seekers—the disciples of Jesus of Nazareth—were transformed into a force that ultimately changed the world. That's the power of the servant-leader model.

Yet few leaders actually "get" and apply it. Paul Martinelli, an associate of John Maxwell, explains why:

> Here's the problem, most organizations operate from a hierarchical leadership structure. Leaders "move up" the ladder in an organization, and, once there, see themselves "above" their team. Despite its trending status—as well as its undeniable success—most people do not equate leadership to service. Rather than epitomizing humility and meeting people where they are at, too many leaders think being a leader means power and authority.[4]

Humble servant leadership should be both strategic and tactical. Align MD's vision required a team of people whose first inclination is service as its own reward. So, I started a nonprofit organization called the Align MD Foundation. We made medical mission trips staffed with doctors, nurses, and medical assistants to Ethiopia, Cambodia, Guatemala, and Haiti. Most of the expenses were paid by the company. When we recruited doctors to join our staff, these trips were one of the first things discussed, to ensure they knew who we were and what we were about. The candidate's reaction was an important part of the hiring decision. Most of the people we ended up hiring said things like, "Yeah, I took a trip to Honduras in medical school" or "I've always wanted to do that!" The humble service mentality was modeled throughout the company.

Tactical humility was a priority at Align MD, as well. Our leaders were not exempt from working the undesirable shifts in the emergency department. I tracked the number of weekend and night shifts, as well as holiday shifts, the team leaders scheduled for themselves and worked, and I also tracked my own. We had no special parking spots for leaders. No leaders were paid extra for the hours spent seeing patients; they got exactly what the other members of their team got. All physicians were expected to pitch in when nursing shortages created bottlenecks in care—meaning if a doctor was the only one available to do the enema a patient needed, he or she did so. And if he was free, the leader did it as an opportunity to serve. Those who felt they were above that kind of service were quickly weeded out. The nursing staff responded very positively to that attitude.

Being a servant leader requires being secure enough to be humble, humble enough to know that you don't know everything, and, most of all, putting the wellbeing of the team before your own selfish desires.

3. Leading Requires Love

People buy into the leader before they buy into the leader's vision. In other words, who the leader is as a person determines the team's level of commitment to his or her vision and the mission.

Nowhere is this truer than in combat. Would you risk your life for a commander you did not respect? Would you voluntarily take extreme personal risks for someone you didn't like, and whom you were convinced didn't care at all for you as a human being? Smart battlefield commanders know positional authority can go only so far. We don't usually think about love in the context of war, but soldiers' willingness to expose themselves to injury or death hinges not only on their love of country, but also on their love and admiration for their commander—and they quickly discern whether their leader cares about them. You've heard the expression, "I'd follow that man to Hell and back." I often ask myself, as a CEO and even now as a congressman, "Who would follow me to Hell and back? Who wouldn't, and why not?"

The battlefield taught me that getting people to buy into me as a leader starts with the principle embedded in a familiar saying: "No one cares how much you know until they know how much you care." That's why I told my managers at Align MD to avoid the trap of proving to everyone how smart they were. That is especially hard for physicians because the road to becoming one is a rigorous challenge that requires clearing a series of hurdles with excellence. People of a certain temperament are drawn to those challenges, and humility isn't always a natural part of that construction. Many docs have attached a significant portion of their identity to their intellect. Nevertheless, our culture made it clear that showing that you genuinely cared for both patients and staff was the top priority. Love the people around you, and those people will love you.

Creating this vital "the commander cares" culture requires engagement, presence, and showing sincere interest in people. A question I often ask prospective new managers is, "What are the names of the children of the two coworkers closest to you in your last job?" If leaders can do that, it's a pretty good indicator that they care about the people around them. That's an indispensable quality in the leaders I look for, because leading requires love. Think of the influence you gain as a leader if you go watch one of your team members' kids' Little League game. Talk about grabbing their heart! Or imagine putting profit behind serving the loved one of someone on your staff—for example, closing shop for the entire team to attend the funeral of a colleague's spouse?

I saw this principal in action shortly after graduating from Ranger School. My first CO was a Vietnam War veteran who was hard, exacting, and mean. He was competent, and the men respected him—but we didn't love him. Eventually, he was replaced by a new battalion commander, Lieutenant Colonel Tom Metz. When he addressed the 850 wild-hearted infantrymen for the first time, he held up a body bag and told us that one of his key personal goals was to never put a soldier in a body bag for any stupid reasons. As he told us this, he got choked up and began to fight back tears. Men generally tend to be uncomfortable about crying in front of each other— especially soldiers, and particularly infantrymen. Nevertheless, as time went by, we grew to understand that he genuinely cared about us as human beings, rather than just seeing us as expendable cogs in a piece of military machinery.

Another time, our unit was deployed to Fort Bragg for field training. After several days of roughing it, eating nothing but field rations, we were unexpectedly called back to our temporary battalion headquarters. When we arrived, we discovered that Metz had gone out, acquired a few whole pigs at his own expense, and was in the process of cooking the meat himself in an inground pit. He proceeded to lay out a barbecue feast that included smoked pork and generous fixings, which he personally served to each of the six hundred men.

That act of love, and others like it, showed us that Metz authentically cared about us. We would have marched into Hell with him.

There are an infinite number of ways to show that you have a heart for your people, but it requires intentionality. At Align MD, we bought food when no one expected it, catered events, rewarded exceptional behavior with spontaneous gifts, celebrated family or life events with our teammates, and many other simple, low-cost actions. Perhaps the greatest way to show your love for people is to fight for them. Invariably there is conflict, and conflict provides an opportunity to teach your staff to serve, and to defend them in front of others as much as you can. ER physicians are often contracted through staffing companies like Align MD. So, when a permanent provider on the medical staff complains to the hospital's decision makers, it puts the contract—often valued at millions of dollars per year—at risk. There is nothing like telling a permanent hospital staff physician or administrator they are going to have to go through you to take action against someone on your team. When your guys are right, defend them publicly. When they're not, discipline them privately.

Metz exemplified love, sacrifice, and service. He taught me that to be the very best servant leader, you have to love the people you are charged with leading. He may have cried when he arrived, but we all cried when he left.

4. Leading Requires Integrity

Integrity is perhaps the most important aspect of creating a winning culture and therefore a successful organization. The laws woven into the fabric of the universe dictate that corruption and dishonesty cannot prosper for long. A culture of integrity begins at the top and flows downward through the organization. Dishonest leaders will produce dishonest followers and a generally corrupt enterprise. No dishonest person can lead a "we before me" team.

I have seen this principle in operation several times. Back at West Point, a mentor, Colonel Tex Turner, shared a personal story from his time in Vietnam that I have never forgotten.

Colonel Tex was an "old school" leader who headed up the Department of Military Science, tasked with teaching us to be warriors and leaders of warriors. I recall he once stabbed a rifle with bayonet affixed into the floor of a building for effect while screaming at the head of a formation of cadets. Tex was a warrior.

As the guest speaker for our company honor class when I was a senior, Tex shared a pivotal story on integrity. A young infantry platoon of thirty combat soldiers had patrolled Vietnam's central highlands all day in 100-degree heat and nearly 100 percent humidity, all while carrying 100 pounds of combat equipment, ammunition, and rations. As twilight approached, the men prepared to hunker down for a miserable night in the bush. The first order of business in bedding down for the night in a combat zone is to dig protective foxholes. But the lieutenant knew the men were exhausted, so he decided to allow them to take a break, eat a meal, and rest first. Around 10:00 p.m., the commander radioed the lieutenant and asked, "Are your men dug in? We expect an enemy attack." The young officer lied. Embarrassed and not wanting to admit that he had allowed the men to skip this basic step, he said, "Yes, we are good to go."

Soon after that radio call, a North Vietnamese company of sixty soldiers attacked. All but one member of the platoon were killed.

Good intentions coupled with a face-saving lie resulted in catastrophe. By the way, the person who related that story to me had been the commander on the other end of that radio. He assured me that if the lieutenant had been honest with him, he would have immediately sent help to get the men dug in and protected for the fight. He also would have relieved that lieutenant of command, but his men most likely would have survived the night. In business, we are often tempted to take shortcuts and fudge the truth, but integrity is essential. Nothing kills the culture of an organization more than an untrustworthy leader. No one gives 110 percent to someone they know lies.

Occasionally, tough love is needed when leading people. Sometimes the right decision will initially be unpopular with the rank and file, like making soldiers dig protective fighting positions before they eat and rest from a long day's march, or working staff longer hours to prepare for that annual inspection or major sales event. That's when it is vital to have previously established a solid level of trust in your integrity and in your concern for the success of the whole team. You can only make a withdrawal from accounts to which you've previously made deposits.

5. Leading Means Facilitating Your People's Best

Whenever I speak to leaders, I often bring one of my Night Stalker challenge coins for a little show-and-tell. Commanders carry coins like these, waiting for just the right opportunity to recognize one of their men for exemplary effort or execution. If he sees a young sergeant giving a particularly outstanding class, on the spot, he will hand him a coin. That coin represents recognition of merit. In the Army, collecting these coins is a real source of pride. I'll admit it, there is a glass-topped coffee table in my congressional office where I display mine.

A spontaneous attaboy/attagirl system is a very powerful thing. In my business, we instituted something called the "U Rock Form": When an ER doc or administrator identified extra effort or excellence, he or she filled out a U Rock Form, gave a copy to the team member, and sent another copy to headquarters. This triggered sending a gift card to the team member being recognized. Reward for merit is a very powerful culture multiplier.

Allowing people to maximize their potential is another major key to success in leadership and involves cultivating a knack for setting people up to succeed rather than to just get by. Satisfaction results when people are doing what God made them to do. Every individual has different skills and personality traits that make them more suited to certain roles than others. Unsurprisingly, most people prefer to do what they do well—and this also benefits the organization.

When a leader invests in identifying and developing every teammate's strengths, the individuals feel appreciated, and the downstream effects include enhanced productivity and reduced turnover.

How can you assess your team members' strengths? There are all sorts of tools you can use to find the best fit for their personality, temperament, and skills. I like the DiSC personal assessment[5] and the Gallup CliftonStrengths tool.[6] Periodic meetings with team members provided an opportunity to talk about that person's specific strengths and how their mix of talents was being utilized. Most of the time when we built leadership teams, we used these tools to map the members' strengths and weaknesses to expose gaps and cover as many different strengths as possible. Some assessment tools even predict where overlap can create communications and partnership challenges. This enabled us to pair people for optimal execution of the team's mission.

The following is an example of such a map for a leadership team covering a Level II trauma center. This is based on Gallup's Strengths assessment listing an individual's top five strengths and the domains of leadership within which those individual strengths fall.

Role	Executing	Influencing	Relationship	Strategic
Medical Director	Achiever, Deliberate, Responsibility	Significance, Self-Assurance		
Assistant Medical Director	Responsibility, Consistent, Discipline		Harmony, Includer	
Nursing Director	Responsibility		Harmony, Restorative, Individualization	Context
Assistant Nursing Director	Focus	Maximizer		Strategic, Ideation, Futuristic

Role	Executing	Influencing	Relationship	Strategic
EMS Director	Achiever	Command	Individualization	Strategic, Learner
Physician's Assistant/ Nurse Practitioner Leader	Achiever, Responsibility		Relator, Developer	Strategic
Staff Assistant	Achiever, Responsibility	Command	Positivity	Learner

Putting your people in places where they can excel is the most important task of a leader, followed by building a team of people whose gifts and talents set them up for success while minimizing conflict.

Facilitating your team's best also requires creating a true meritocracy in your organization—a culture in which talent, hard work, initiative, diligence, and other key virtues can be rewarded. If you don't measure results at both the individual and team level, how will you know whether a member is flourishing or floundering? How can you know if you have someone in the right spot?

Of course, hiring, rewarding, and promoting based on merit has fallen out of fashion in recent times. We've raised a generation or two on the "participation trophy" system. That's a system in which kids receive the message that excelling doesn't bring rewards because it might hurt the feelings of those who either didn't have as much talent or didn't put in the hard hours of training and skill-building required to excel.

Today we have those who would extend the participation-trophy mindset to all the systems of our culture—including academics and the marketplace. In 2021, the Virginia Department of Education decided to drop its accelerated math programs in the name of "equity."[7] That word doesn't mean "equality of opportunity"—a level playing field for all participants; it means "equality of outcome" irrespective of talent, aptitude, dedication, or effort. Here is the problem: Ending rewards for extraordinary achievement destroys the incentives for individuals to go the extra mile. Leaders must be free to reward those who do what's necessary to be really good at what they do, and those who achieve excellence must be free to enjoy those rewards. It comes back to freedom.

Let me offer one last suggestion about placing people where it's best for them and the organization: Hiring leaders means much more than just hiring someone with the skills and personality for a team. When you trust someone to lead your organization or team, he or she becomes an extension of your company, department, or unit. Each company should define the set of values most essential to accomplish the vision. If you can organize those values in an acronym or pneumonic for all to know and remember easily, it further reenforces them. For example, the Army's seven core values are articulated with the acronym LDRSHIP. For leaders at Align MD, I used the pneumonic FAITH. The "F" stands for "faith"; I wanted our leaders to really believe in our vision. The "A" is for "available." Real leaders need bandwidth to meet their people's needs. The "I" stands for "innovation"; if you are not an "ideas person," it's really hard to lead organizations where problems require quick solutions. "T" represents "teachable." Ray Kroc, the iconic businessman who took McDonald's from a mom-and-pop operation to a global multinational corporation once said, "As long as you're green, you're growing. As soon as you're ripe, you start to rot."[8] Everyone needs to have a learning mindset. The "H" stands for "honesty."

6. Leaders Must Be Seen

There are many bosses but very few leaders. Leadership is no easy mantle to assume. But then, important things are rarely easy. As we've seen, leading well requires:

- A humble servant's heart,
- Genuine concern for the individuals you lead,
- An authentic sense of personal integrity,
- A commitment to seeing those you lead find their optimum place of contribution and enjoy the rewards they truly merit, and
- That you are present and responsive.

This attitude is crucial to absorb at the cellular level, because the leader sets the tone for everyone in the organization. Each day the leader fails to do so is a day lost. When "we before me" becomes part of the organization's DNA, there is virtually nothing that team cannot accomplish. Please note, this can only come from the top down. You have to model it. As the old saying goes, some things are more easily caught than taught.

In the Army, there are some colorful ways soldiers mock leaders who don't lead with a "we before me" ethic. For example, former infantrymen may be familiar with the acronym REMF: The "RE" stands for "rear echelon," a fancy term for the safety and comfort to be found at the back of the battle formation. (For decorum's sake, I'll let you guess what the "MF" represents.) If a commander is labeled a "REMF," it suggests that he is never up forward with the troops, enduring the same hardships and deprivations as those in the front lines.

I've never understood managers or executives who think they can lead from their corner offices, but I've seen several of them. If you are not spending a healthy amount of time in the foxhole, on the factory floor, in the intensive care unit, or at the point of customer engagement, your "troops" know it. The unit is watching. If you're in a position of leadership or management and you're not applying the principles I've outlined above, you are very likely perceived as a REMF. And that is holding your entire organization back.

One last word on this. My time in the Army introduced me to phenomenal leaders like General Gary Luck, Lieutenant General Tom Metz, Major General Clay Hutmacher, and many others. Jeff Colt, now a retired major general, was the commander to whom I reported when I joined the 160th Night Stalkers. He, too, was one of the greatest leaders I ever worked for, primarily because he exemplified all the "we before me" values I just laid out. He always put himself last. He deeply understood the ancient wisdom of "he who would be the greatest among you must be the servant of all." Colt placed himself between the Army senior leadership and his soldiers. He, and maybe one other leader in my entire career, stood up to the stupid missions that infrequently come down from on high, where the reality of the picture on the ground is often lost. He took that risk to his career and livelihood so his warriors did not have to take unnecessary risks in combat or peacetime. He eschewed the perks and privileges of rank. He led by serving his men. And every single one of them would willingly follow him to Hell and back.

May each of the people within our spheres of influence say the same of you and me.

CHAPTER 6

Toward a More Perfect Union

How "We Before Me" Can Rescue Our Families

It is not money, but the family that is the foundation
of public life. As it has become weaker, every structure
built upon that foundation has become weaker.

—James Q. Wilson

Any book about how to restore our great nation through the principles of "we before me" would be remiss to avoid talking about the state of the American family—the most basic building block of our society. And the sad fact of the matter is, right now, it's struggling. To address the issues of what's wrong with our families, we must begin by addressing the state of our marriages.

We spend a lot of time teaching kids how to drive before we hand them a license and leave them alone behind the wheel of a car. But as a culture, we don't teach young people anything at all before handing them a marriage license. As a result, most of us enter marriage clueless about what it will be like and what success will require. That was certainly true for Camie and me, and it showed. We had some rough patches early in our marriage. Most couples do.

In today's politically correct, gender-neutral world, acknowl-
edging differences between men and women, even within marriage,
often creates a battle, but Camie and I fit the traditional molds. Like
most guys, I wanted to solve all her problems and, more often than
not, she just wanted me to listen when she talked about them. There
were also the differences inherent in our personalities, most notably,
my extroversion versus her introversion. With some counseling and
a trip through the Myers-Briggs Personality Type Inventory, we
learned that like most extroverts, I think out loud, but Camie would
often interpret my thoughts as plans. The lack of details in my voiced
ideas made my free-flowing thoughts difficult for both of us. (Lesson:
Extroverts should make sure they tell someone who might interpret
their thoughts as plans that they are just thinking out loud.)

Perhaps our greatest struggle was understood best after Camie
and I both took the Gallup Strengths assessment. The results were
eye-opening. Almost all of Camie's strengths lie in the relational
domain, while mine are in the strategic domain. And each of our
strengths were the areas where the other was weakest—or as author
John Maxwell refers to them, "blind spots." For me, learning to be
relational in the way Camie needed has always been a challenge; I
simply do not think the way she does. And since I am strategic and
extroverted, I would compound the differences by rattling off another
great idea in an effort to fix our problem that Camie thought she, as
a detail-oriented person, had to help execute. It was a toxic cocktail!
The survey equipped us to solve our problems by seeing them for what
they were: We each brought different strengths and subsequently blind
spots to the partnership.

But it was hard. About four years into the marriage, we asked
ourselves the hard question: *Do we quit?* We were disillusioned.

The bridge of disillusionment is a very useful metaphor from
Christian author Skip Gray. In a presentation I attended, he spoke

about the Apostle Peter's great failure—his triple denial of his friend and leader, Jesus—and the resulting crisis of confidence it triggered in him. Peter thought he knew himself and what his values were. But in the moment of testing, he folded like a lawn chair. He wasn't the rock of strength and courage he thought he was, nor that his mentor had predicted he would be.

The profound shame and self-disappointment undid him. He basically quit the life of discipleship he had been leading and went back to his old life of fishing. Only a revelatory reconciliation with the One he'd disappointed could put Peter back on the path to his destiny (see Matthew 26:69–75).

"The road to maturity," Gray said, "requires crossing the bridge of disillusionment." Peter became one of the greatest apostles who built the Christian church by pushing across the bridge, not quitting—maturing as a leader and becoming a seminal figure in the greatest movement in human history.

The journey of life tends to lead all of us onto the bridge of disillusionment at various points. For me, that greatest disillusionment was the trouble Camie and I experienced in the early years of marriage. At a particularly difficult point for us, I was listening to the words of a song by Lifehouse, "Whatever It Takes." The song is about a couple in trouble, with the artist lamenting how he has hurt his partner. The poignant section was the artist's simple commitment, "But if you can find a reason to stay, I'll do whatever it takes to turn this around."[1]

"Whatever it takes." That is the determined selflessness of "we before me." Like my dad driving nails with the palm of his one hand, whatever it takes.

I'm so thankful Camie and I both chose to cross the bridge of disillusionment together and reach a maturity in our relationship that is incredibly fulfilling. She's has been a wonderful life partner and has played an indispensable role in everything we've accomplished so far and will accomplish going forward.

The solution for us came with (mostly) patient education of each other regarding our differences. But the starting point was learning to live out the actual meaning of the words "I love you." There are three words for love in the Greek language: *agape*, *eros*, and *phileo*. Each carries different meanings that are all important in marriage: *Eros* (from which we get the word "erotic") is self-explanatory. *Phileo* means the kinship of brotherly love. And *agape* is sacrificial love, like when someone gives their life to save someone else's. Whatever it takes—"we before me."

In a practical sense, overcoming our marital challenges required recognizing and understanding how God made both Camie and me. In the end, resolving those issues came down to better communication, as most issues of conflict do. And what got us through it all was putting our marriage ("we") ahead of ourselves individually.

■ ■ ■

For a long time, sociological research has revealed that half of all American marriages end in divorce. If that figure has dropped, it is only because fewer young people are bothering to get married at all. And given that the family is the fundamental building block of a stable, prosperous society, that's not a good thing.

In their book *Saving Your Marriage Before It Starts*, professional marriage counselors Drs. Les and Leslie Parrott point to unrealistic expectations as a key cause of marriage trouble and failure. Referring to their own struggles in their first year, they wrote:

> Not that we were in serious trouble. But we had this naïve idea that after our wedding our life would fall naturally

into place, and a marriage preparation course or counseling never entered our minds.... We simply thought we would tie the proverbial knot, set up house, and as the fairy tales say, "live happily ever after."[2]

The Parrots' workbook has become one of the bestselling marriage preparation guides of the last thirty years. In their own words, they wrote it "to take the mythology out of marriage. For too long, marriage has been saddled with unrealistic expectations and misguided assumptions."[3] Take note of the terminology there: "mythology." "Unrealistic expectations." "Misguided assumptions." Although they don't use the phrase, they are clearly articulating the concept of the bridge of disillusionment.

I suspect that a major reason many marriages flounder is that our current culture doesn't teach determined selflessness. Actually, it teaches us the opposite. Most people have been raised to think that their own needs and desires are paramount. We enter marriage trained to focus on what will make us happy, rather than how to focus on the happiness of our spouse and the wellbeing of the union. In fact, a new trend concludes that if "it doesn't make me happy, it's actually wrong for me to do it"; therefore, if we are not happy, we are morally *obligated* to get the heck out of the marriage. That's crazy!

Athletes, medical students, military units, and many other groups all recognize that challenges make a person and a team stronger and better. In those contexts, we call it "resilience." Like the player recruited to play quarterback who gets shifted to tight end for the sake of the team, resilience is a willingness to make personal changes for the sake of the team in order to win the game. Marriage is the same.

Selflessness and resilience don't come naturally to any human being, but can be learned. Marriage and family therapist Dr. Greg Smalley says it this way:

Learn to make sacrifices. The ultimate weapon against selfishness is sacrifice, and a happy marriage is often predicated on two people trying to out-serve each other.... The fight against selfishness means shelving the "me" and stressing the "we." Make sure that your marriage has room for *both* of you: Embrace your interdependence—your inherent need and love for each other.[4]

Sound familiar? He's speaking the language of "we before me." It's a philosophical approach that makes any institution or organization that involves more than one person stronger and healthier, families most of all.

Disillusionment and disappointment drive a lot of marital trouble. Too many couples either stay stuck on that bridge or jump off. However, the road to maturity requires crossing the bridge of disillusionment. Camie and I can personally testify that on the other side lies a deep, rich, rewarding relationship. It doesn't mean marriage gets easier—it just means your bonds and your identity as a partner in the marriage are strengthened, and your growth as a person and a team become exponential. So, in a sense, "we before me" becomes both the means and the end of sticking to it and getting to the other side.

There's something much larger at stake here. If we're going to get serious about restoring American greatness, we'll have to start with restoring not just marriages, but the whole family as well.

■ ■ ■

There are a host of reasons families are struggling, but one of the main ones is that for the last sixty years, government has been intruding into this sacred territory. In 1965, the late U.S. Senator Daniel Patrick Moynihan (D-NY), alarmed by a disturbing amount of fatherlessness among black children in urban areas, published "The Moynihan Report," in which he detailed the problems he saw: poor education, poor health, and poverty in general.[5] The Johnson administration then used that report to massively expand the federal government's reach through "the Great Society"—a host of new taxpayer-funded programs that are still in operation today: Medicare, Medicaid, funding for government-run schools, and welfare programs to address poverty in both urban and rural areas.

While these programs have accomplished a great amount of good, flooding those issues with cash did not solve the problems; rather, it multiplied many of them.

In their meticulously researched book *American Restoration: How Faith, Family, and Personal Sacrifice Can Heal Our Nation* (Washington, D.C.: Regnery Gateway, 2019), Timothy S. Goeglein and Craig Osten show that the issues urban black families in America faced in the mid-1960s are now decimating families of all races nationwide. And the key to all of this is marriage.

Let's look at a few statistics:

- The federal government launched the Aid to Families of Dependent Children (AFDC) program in 1935. By 1960, only 4 percent of the children receiving welfare had mothers who'd never been married (the rest were widows, etc.). By 1996, two-thirds of the children receiving aid had mothers who'd never been married.[6]
- In 1965, 25 percent of black children nationwide were living in fatherless households. In 2014, 70 percent of black children nationwide were born out of wedlock, as were more than half of Hispanic children and one-third of white children.[7]

- In 1970, only 15 percent of all American babies (all racial groups combined) were born out of wedlock. By 2014, 65.7 percent of American babies born to women under the age of 25, and 37.7 percent born to women between the ages of 25 and 29, were born out of wedlock. The overall out-of-wedlock birth rate was 40.2 percent, which held steady through 2018.[8]
- In 1970, there were 77 marriages for every 1,000 women age 15 or older; by 2015, that number had dropped to 32 marriages per 1,000 women age 15 or older—the lowest rate in American history.[9]
- According to the National Longitudinal Survey of Youth, a 10 percent increase in welfare benefits increased by 12 percent the odds that a young woman (under the age of 22) will have a child out of wedlock. This effect was consistent across racial lines.[10]

In a 2018 article published in *National Affairs*, author Mary Eberstadt summed up this correlation neatly: "Economists are fond of saying if we want more of something, we should subsidize it. And, though it's been done with the best intentions, that is exactly what the welfare state has been doing across the free societies of the West: subsidizing family breakdown."[11]

And the deleterious effects of that breakdown continue to spiral outward, continuing to affect individual families for generations at a stretch, thus leaving society at large poorer—figuratively and literally—for the experience. For example:

- Black boys who grow up in fatherless homes are twice as likely to go to jail as those who grow up in two-parent households.[12]

- Fatherless girls often become "severely depressed, self-destructive, and sexually promiscuous as they seek to fill the void left by the absence of a loving father."[13]
- Fatherless boys tend to deal with that void through anger and rage—including mass shootings.[14]
- Numerous studies have shown that children in single-parent homes are more likely to engage in substance abuse than those in stable, two-parent homes.[15]

Though 80 percent of black children being raised by single mothers live at or below the poverty line, less than 10 percent of black children with married parents do.[16] But it is not merely the presence of a man in the home that makes the critical difference: According to the U.S. Census Bureau, as of 2021, data showed that children living with two parents who were cohabiting instead of married were about as likely to experience poverty as those raised by single mothers.[17]

Thus it is marriage—not race—that makes the critical difference in childhood outcomes on virtually every level. In fact,

> Scarcely any area of public policy is unaffected by the decline in marriage and family life. Educational attainment of children outside of marriage suffers, the job teachers face is more complicated, and crime is connected with fatherlessness.... As the family declines, the state rises to take its place; as the state rises to take its place, the family declines further.[18]

Elsewhere in this book, we've touched briefly on the riots that engulfed our nation during the summer of 2020. Several factors contributed to those riots, but underneath all of them was the growing sense of cultural hegemony—the Marxist principle of "the haves vs.

the have-nots" in society—that boiled over into abject rage, resulting in widespread looting and vandalism. While we can debate those issues at another time, in a sense, there is a very real caste system now operating in our nation, but its foundation is not race, religion, or sexuality, as certain activists would have us believe. Rather, it is the gulf "between those who are born healthy and are nurtured in a two-parent home, and those who emerge from the womb with three strikes already against them: drug-addicted, trapped in poverty, and lacking an essential parent," Goeglein and Osten write.[19]

> We are left, then, with a society where intact families are not the norm but are something of a luxury good. That's hardly a healthy foundation.[20]

Science strongly suggests that the antidote to this downward spiral of family dissolution is faith and church attendance. Why? One study from Harvard University researchers

> surmises it's because religious teachings are sacred, an important bond is created in the marriage vows, and attending religious services reinforces that bond. Religious teachings across all faiths discourage divorce and have strong teachings against adultery. They also provide family support through connections with other families, and perhaps most important, place a strong emphasis on love and putting the needs of others above one's own.[21]

That is the very essence of "we before me." The nation is stuck on a bridge of disillusionment (in some cases rage), and it is partly our own fault. Disincentivizing marriage has disadvantaged those born outside it; the data is clear. However, on the individual level, doing "whatever it takes"—putting the whole marriage and family ahead of self—can save us. If enough couples do so, we will walk the nation across the bridge together.

CHAPTER 7

To Cross the Great Divide
"We Before Me" Can Unite Our Nation

*Darkness cannot drive out darkness: only light can do
that. Hate cannot drive out hate: only love can do that.*

—Martin Luther King Jr.

I'll never forget the first chest I "cracked" in the emergency department as a resident. That probably warrants an explanation.

Whenever a patient arrives at the emergency department under specific criteria following penetrating trauma to the chest, the ER doc will in rare instances cut through the sternum to separate the two halves of the ribcage, exposing the lungs and heart. In this case, a black father was walking his son to school when a black assailant grabbed his son's backpack. The honorable dad chased the thief around a corner, where the assailant was waiting with a large Bowie knife. He stabbed the man under his left armpit and into the left ventricle of his heart. I plugged the tear in the heart with a balloon catheter before sending him to the operating room for emergency surgery. After my shift, I went upstairs to the OR to check on him. He had not survived.

A year later, in my last year of training as an emergency medicine resident, the same kind of case came before me. A white soldier was injured in a training exercise, and once again, we cracked the chest. That patient did not survive, either.

In both cases, the blood on the floor was the same color red and the hearts I held in my hand were nearly identical. Certainly, there were no signs of the individual's race beneath the skin. A military leader once said, "On the battlefield, we all bleed red." As a physician who treated combat casualties in Iraq and Afghanistan, I can tell you that leader was 100 percent correct.

I shared earlier about my parents' efforts to teach my siblings and I that the different races have equal value before God and therefore should have equal value before man. Perhaps that's why Dr. Martin Luther King dreamed of a society that looked at character and not skin color. But despite my upbringing, I was still aware of racism. In fact, I protested once in high school against a community leader who failed to invite black students to an event. Fast-forward to Congress, when I said something nice on social media about Congressman Elijah Cummings when he died, and a constituent told me I had just lost his vote. I have no illusions about the fact that there is still some deeply entrenched racial prejudice in our great country.

But over the time I've been alive, something has happened in America. The year 2020 brought a lot of long-simmering racial tensions to a rolling boil. The issues are complex and beyond the scope of this book, but I have frequently observed that black and white Americans remind me in some ways of a couple on the verge of divorce in an arranged marriage that history forced upon them many generations ago.

As a society, we're on the bridge of disillusionment in several respects and must find a way to cross over. Many older Americans, both black and white, remember the heroic efforts to end segregation and legally sanctioned discrimination in the 1950s and '60s. Those efforts resulted in real, meaningful victories, including the *Brown v. Board of Education* ruling at the U.S. Supreme Court in 1954, the Civil Rights Act of 1964, and the Voting Rights Act of 1965. Many people saw those hard-won victories as the gateway to higher living standards and better outcomes for the next generation of black Americans. And for many, they were. A black middle class emerged and grew throughout the 1970s, '80s, and into the '90s—so much so that the left-leaning Brookings Institute observed in a 1998 report:

> Progress is the largely suppressed story of race and race relations over the past half-century. And thus, it's news that more than 40 percent of African Americans now consider themselves members of the middle class. Forty-two percent own their own homes, a figure that rises to 75 percent if we look just at black married couples.[1]

	About 10	About 100	About 1,000	About 10,000	More than 10,000
Individual Estimates of the Number of Black Men Shot Annually by Law Enforcement in America					
Very Liberal	15.71%	30.71%	31.43%	14.29%	7.86%
Liberal	22.42%	38.79%	26.67%	6.67%	5.45%
Moderate	33.60%	40.59%	16.40%	5.91%	3.49%
Conservative	46.39%	40.36%	9.04%	3.01%	1.20%
Very Conservative	45.99%	33.58%	13.14%	2.92%	4.38%

Source: Skeptic Research Center[2]

Nevertheless, more than two and a half decades later, a significant number of people sincerely believe little progress has been made at all. A survey performed as a part of the Civil Unrest and Presidential Election Study reveals just how far perceptions are from reality: When asked to select options on a multiple-choice test for the number of black people killed by police, most people guessed high.

More than half of those who identify as "very liberal" believe the numbers are about or greater than 1,000. More than 20 percent say it's at least 10,000 per year. Slightly more than 20 percent of moderates believe the number is more than 100 times greater than the actual number, which is around ten black men shot by police every year. Even the conservative and very conservative believe the number is about 1,000 times greater than it actually is. How can they all be so wrong?

This is disillusionment and disappointment—or at a minimum, disinformation—on a massive scale. I am not in any way asserting racism's ills have been expelled from the country—in fact, just the opposite. Therefore, it's no surprise that our national racial "marriage" is in jeopardy. Just as everyone loses in marital divorce, especially younger and future generations, it's clear to me that there can be no American renewal or renaissance without fixing *this* marriage.

■ ■ ■

Of course, I'm aware than any attempt to tackle this issue is fraught with peril. I'm not sure whether I'm being brave or foolish here, but I can't help but try. I genuinely have a heart to see racial reconciliation in our country.

The boundaries of my congressional district mean I represent downtown Nashville, Tennessee, as well as the people living in hundreds of small towns, some of which are home to black churches. My role in Congress gives me the pleasure of knowing and speaking to both black and white pastors, recording artists, and key figures in the entertainment industry.

One of the many wonderful things about the mutual trust and goodwill that comes from real relationships is the freedom to speak your heart, hear the other person's perspective, perhaps still see things differently, and yet walk away as friends. This is why the ideological self-segregation that Americans have been engaging in over the last thirty years creates enormous challenges to our society. It's profoundly healthy to have friends and acquaintances who don't see the world the same way you do. Yet, the more polarized and insulated we get, the more our tribes encourage us to cut everyone else out of our lives.

I never fail to learn something or better understand a different viewpoint when I have a real conversation with one of my black friends. For example, in the middle of one of the past waves of protest over an officer-involved shooting of a black person, I was having lunch with a pastor friend. I had observed in several places within the black community a strong negative reaction to the statement "*All* lives matter." I was genuinely curious about it, so I asked, "What's wrong with saying, 'All lives matter'? Why is that offensive? It's true, isn't it?"

Because he and I have a real relationship, with deposits of good-will and good faith on reserve on both sides, he patiently explained how that statement hits the ears of a black person who is trying to draw attention to what he or she believes is an ongoing pattern of injustice against black people by law enforcement. He helped me see it from his perspective. I didn't fully buy into every single one of the premises and assumptions underlying his position, but I still gained empathy and sensitivity. And my friend appreciated my willingness to listen.

I then asked if I could share how I, as a combat veteran, feel when I see professional athletes kneeling while the national anthem plays.

He said, "Of course." I spoke of the friends and colleagues I'd served alongside who'd made the ultimate sacrifice in order to preserve liberty and confront tyranny. I explained, as best I could, the bravery, sacrifice, and honor I'd seen men and women of every color and creed display, and how they felt when they saw that star-spangled banner waving. I talked about the flag-draped coffins I'd seen and the meticulously folded flags I myself had given to young widows with small children. I spoke of my father, whose service had ultimately cost him his arm. I reminded my friend that the first black person to win the Medal of Honor did so by saving the United States flag after the flag-bearer was shot during the Civil War. I shared how hurtful and offensive it feels when athletes protest law enforcement policies by targeting the symbol of American freedom—especially given that policing is essentially a *local* issue, and the anthem is national.

He heard me. He might not have fully bought into all of the premises and assumptions underlying my position, either, but he still gained empathy and sensitivity, and I appreciated his willingness to listen. Our friendship was stronger for the conversation.

Unfortunately, most discussions about race in America amount to angry factions talking past each other, echoing the latest talking points handed down by partisans with huge platforms. Often, white people sincerely interested in having a real conversation are told they simply need to be quiet and listen. Yet, there's no relationship if only one side is allowed to share thoughts and feelings. That's a monologue, not a dialogue. If this arranged marriage is going to work, both parties are going to have to be willing to listen—*and* speak.

I discussed in the last chapter how after a few years of marriage, Camie and I realized we had some real communications issues that needed improvement. So we saw a counselor to help us learn how better to talk with and listen to one another. Too often, it seemed we were speaking different languages. You may recall the bestselling 1992 book *Men Are from Mars, Women Are from Venus,* which documented the many ways men and women process information differently. In light of that reality, often I would proudly give what I thought to be the perfect response to Camie at a sensitive moment, only to quickly realize that what I said had made matters worse. I thought I was clearly saying one thing, yet she heard something quite different.

We see a similar dynamic when a white guy says "all lives matter" in the middle of a debate on racial profiling by police. I was recently informed that when some black people hear white politicians say they "want to go back to the way it was," they assume these leaders mean going back to the time when Jim Crow laws were preeminent, when most often what the speaker means is that they want to see our country return to a time when power was still distributed more among the states than in Washington, prices were lower, and the media was merely informative rather than weaponized. No one has ever said, "Hey, let's resurrect Jim Crow laws!" It is tragic that some black leaders believe this is what we're proposing. But there are also plenty of leaders who disingenuously make these claims because they themselves will gain power, votes, and—yes—money when others believe them. Plenty of people are profiting from negative stereotypes. (If you believe black people are incapable of getting an ID in order to vote, you are reinforcing a stereotype. Stop it.)

Applying "we before me" here means we try to use phraseology that works for both parties, the way a husband and wife would. At a minimum, we should not assume the other speaker has ill intent; when they say something that sounds inflammatory, just ask for clarification.

To be honest, I'm not sure how we do marriage counseling as white and black America. As I listen, I hear very real pain in the voices of some of my black friends. One black pastor shared a story about counseling a fifty-year-old black woman with depression and addiction issues. In his session with her, she broke down in tears and said she believed she could never accomplish anything because she was black. She genuinely believed she had no value and nothing to offer society. As often happens, the person most instrumental in convincing her of this was her own father, who was black. He had taught her these poisonous beliefs, and for almost all of her life she had been unable to escape them. The primary thing holding this woman back was her own perception of her identity.

Tragically, there actually are white people who believe they are better than others simply because they are white. Black supremacy is also real, and there are organizations that advance both these fallacies. Like terrorist organizations, both groups recruit disturbed and disaffected people and spread their hatred online.

At the same time, the commonly repeated mantra that "all cops are bad" because unarmed black men are shot by police is a significant reach. According to the FBI, in 2019, black men, who comprise 6 percent of the U.S. population, committed 50 percent of the murders in this country.[3] But a deeper dive shows about 88 percent of black men who were murdered were killed by other black men, and about 81 percent of murdered white people were killed by white men.[4] Admittedly, this uses 2019 data—but that's because it's the last year I could find in my research that broke down the data in a "who kills whom" kind of way; now the FBI just lists the numbers and races of murdered people, which makes the data easier to manipulate by those with an agenda. But the 2019 data strongly suggest that black people are killing black people, and white people are killing white people.

Broad-brush statistics ignore a lot of relevant detail. For example, there is substantial data to suggest unionized police forces kill unarmed minorities at a substantially higher rate than nonunionized police forces.[5] It seems that bad cops, whether white or black, are protected by unions. The white Minnesota police officer who held

George Floyd under his knee for nearly nine minutes never should have been on duty in the first place. He had eighteen complaints, seventeen internal affairs investigations, and two suspicious killings on his record, yet the union kept him on the beat despite the chief's desire to fire him.[6] So do these tragic events stem from systemic racism, or from that union doing what unions occasionally have done in protecting their least effective and most incompetent members? In this case, those being protected are bad cops who may or may not be racist. We need to dig into this more and not just make assumptions based on misused statistics and superficial conclusions that conveniently fit a preferred narrative.

Assuming someone is racist because they are white is itself racist. Assuming all cops are racists is also a form of bias that misrepresents the vast majority of servant-hearted "we before me" police officers. Going this route is a lot like crying wolf, desensitizing people to the cry of genuine racism and diluting the force of the criticism true white supremacy deserves.

I am also aware of the flip side of the coin: Countless white and Asian Americans have felt the system was stacked against them when preferential treatment in hiring or college admissions was given to others based on race. If you are a white male or Asian female applying to medical school with scores that put you in the seventy-fifth percentile, and you discover that a black woman with scores and performance that put her in the fifty-fifth percentile was accepted while you were not, you might get frustrated. That has happened to several of my friends. Injustice is injustice. And whether it is a response to perceived injustices, an ingrained untruth, or a genuine belief that black is better than white or white is better than black, the end result is division, me before we, and societal destruction. What we must do first is listen with a grace-giving, "we before me" mindset—to *everyone*.

These kinds of empathy-cultivating conversations are vital, yet increasingly difficult to have. Why? Because we're increasingly isolated into hardened tribal bubbles constructed of confirmation bias. And there is a multimillion-dollar cottage industry telling all of us we are far more racist than we really are, hence the wildly false perceptions in the table above. We need to get back to the facts.

Perhaps an absurd example can help illustrate a very real truth about confirmation bias. If a person from Mars meets ten people from Venus, and every one of those individuals hates strawberry milkshakes, the Martian, understandably, might form an opinion (or bias) that people from Venus all hate strawberry milkshakes. The next time that Martian encountered a new person from Venus, he might just assume that person hates strawberry milkshakes. This would happen because brains are automatic pattern-recognition machines. Confirmation bias takes this a step further. As the Martian meets others from Venus who do like strawberry milkshakes, the Martian might reject that information as false, or simply fail to notice it. Why? Because the bias formed from previous learning or experience keeps him or her from seeing or accepting the new reality.

Today, some of us have strapped on tribal lenses that make it impossible to see any event objectively. For some, it's the lens of identity politics and Critical Race Theory that sees "whiteness" as the root of evil. For others, it's the lens of perpetual victimhood and entitlement, which causes them to draw conclusions about people as a group. For some, it's the lens of murky, internet-driven conspiracy theories. For others, it's the lens of the Marxist obsession with wealth distribution, identified in the Ten Commandments as covetousness. All of them distort reality and make it nearly impossible to see things through another person's eyes. All of them push us into "us versus them" corners.

"We before me" compels people to listen and assess everyone fairly regardless of the color of their skin, their political affiliation, or what planet they come from. "We before me" listens to understand and not just to rebut. "We before me" also verifies facts in an age of media-generated hyperbole meant to stir up fear and outrage. "We before me," like a married couple, uses language that works for the hearer and not the speaker. "We before me" places the whole above self to the point that it is okay if someone disagrees with us.

But that is where the ideological divide comes in—the topic of the next chapter.

CHAPTER 8

The Rest of the Story

How "We Before Me" Works across All Divisive Issues

With malice toward none, with charity for all, with firmness in the right as God gives us to see the right, let us strive on to finish the work we are in, to bind up the nation's wounds, to care for him who shall have borne the battle and for his widow and his orphan, to do all which may achieve and cherish a just and lasting peace among ourselves and with all nations.

—Abraham Lincoln, Second Inaugural Address

Lincoln spoke the words above in a noble attempt to pour healing balm onto the wounds of a nation torn asunder by war. No, we've not just come through another bloody Civil War that claimed more than 700,000 lives and maimed countless others, but we have been at war with ourselves nonetheless—fighting along political, ideological, educational, geographic, demographic, religious, and, sadly, racial lines. Once we understand the sources and magnifiers of the division, it's easy to see how the principles of "we before me" can solve it.

Americans have always held strong views on a few public policy issues, historically the ones our political parties tended to coalesce around—yet we generally held common values and shared compatible worldviews for most of the last two centuries. That is no longer the case, and our political divisions are growing as our ideologies diverge. Until recently, Americans were also likely to live near and work with people who held views different from their own. Life tended to give us lots of opportunities to be reminded that people who think differently from us are human, too. This has been changing as well, in ways that can actually be measured.

Psychologist Matt Motyl has been tracking and analyzing America's increasing polarization for more than a decade. He points out that as recently as 1992, most Americans lived in counties in which no single political party was overwhelmingly dominant.[1] But since then, we've been rapidly segregating along ideological lines.

In fact, Motyl has been able to create a stunning county-by-county illustration of this thirty-year trend. Counties that voted for the Republican presidential candidate by a margin of 20 percent or greater over the years were colored red; those that voted for the Democrat by 20 percent or more were colored blue; and those in which the election margin was less than 20 percent either way were colored white. One glance at the 1992 map shows most American counties were white, with only a scattering of "homogeneous" red and blue counties. By the 2000 election, the map had filled in with red and blue fairly dramatically. This trend continued and accelerated in the elections of 2004, 2008, and 2012. By 2016, nearly all of the white had disappeared from the map.

This tells us that, as a nation, we are self-segregating into geographical enclaves, and rarely engage on a meaningful level with people who don't agree with our views. That, coupled with our new-found ability to curate our news in a way that allows us to hear only viewpoints that align with our preferred narrative means that most Americans find it increasingly easy to view themselves as "right" and all those who disagree with them as stupid, crazy, evil, or some combination of the three.

If our great-great-grandparents could visit our time, one of the first questions they might ask would be, "When did politics become everyone's all-consuming obsession?" Politics now seeps into and colors virtually every aspect of our lives—from corporate culture to entertainment. For a short time, sports served as our last refuge, a place where people of all persuasions could come together and root for their team and trash-talk the other side. But even that has succumbed to the gravitational pull of polarization in recent years.

How did previous generations have the luxury of not having to think about politics every waking moment? Because government was much smaller and less intrusive back then. Beginning with the passage of a constitutional amendment establishing the federal income tax in 1913, the size, scope, and power of the U.S. government began swelling and has never stopped. The bigger and less constrained the national government got, the more power it took for itself to pick winners and losers in our economy. Both Congress and unelected federal bureaucrats began to wield the power to destroy whole industries with the stroke of a pen. Legislators with utopian impulses learned they could play at social engineering using the tax code—rewarding some behaviors and punishing others, and impacting our lives in profound and lasting ways—sometimes unintentionally (which means, sometimes intentionally). Centralized government in far-off Washington drives the divide as bureaucrats impart their "wisdom" on how Americans should live. Who gets the angriest about that, of course, depends on who holds the power at the time.

Our republic was not designed to function this way. In fact, Americans fought a war to throw off that kind of top-down rule from power centralized in a monarchy. The resulting Tenth Amendment states that if a particular power or authority is not expressly assigned to the federal government in the U.S. Constitution, that power belongs to the states. To get around that nasty and unwanted Tenth Amendment, self-righteous and sometimes well-meaning legislators who favor centralized power in a strong federal government have passed laws in areas where the federal government has no constitutional authority—like education and speed limits on the highway. Worse still, unelected federal bureaucrats create regulations—too many times with no congressional authority, and often resulting in felonies for citizens.

The result has been an increasing sense that the federal government is encroaching on freedom—which means people on both sides of the divide fight harder for control in Washington. The power struggle only worsens the division as it solidifies the battlelines. Just look at what happens when a new president is elected: Upon taking office, he passes executive orders because Congress is at a stalemate. Those executive orders drive the country to that president's way of thinking; the other side seethes in anger. Then, the other party wins the election, and executive orders again flow, reversing the executive orders of the previous administration, and the other side seethes in anger.

We also see it in the selection of federal judges. There was a day in America when competence was all that mattered. Now, with some on the courts interpreting the Constitution not by what it actually says, but by what they think it ought to say, judges are in a position to legislate from the bench. No wonder the confirmation of a Supreme Court justice is the greatest battle of all in Washington.

But more is driving our division than big government in Washington; social and traditional news media play an increasing caustic role, too. The Brookings Institute summarized multiple studies showing social media's measurable effect on division.[2] The American Economic Association compared people's attitudes before and after taking a thirty-day break from Facebook, and found that it increased the amount of time the subjects spent talking in person, decreased their polarization, and not surprisingly, improved their sense of wellbeing.[3]

Traditional news media runs on fear and outrage. Looking specifically at the *New York Times*, Johan Berger and Katherine Milkman of the University of Pennsylvania conducted a study to determine what makes online content go viral.[4] Anger beat all the other emotions, with "awe" and "practical value" tying for second. And that study was published in 2011—practically ancient history after all that's transpired over the last few years. But traditional media's goal is still to grab our attention in the midst of information saturation—now more than ever. Daniel Lattier, writing for the Federation for Economic Education, summarizes it well: "The mainstream news media would have you believe they are just reporting on the anger out there. But they are actually creating it and fomenting it.... They need it to survive."[5]

Unfortunately, the government and media are just tapping our hidden tendencies as humans. Motyl did a great job of explaining the trends I'm describing in an article for CivilPolitics.org highlighting a logical fallacy called "naive realism": It's a tendency to be (falsely) confident that we see events, people, and the world as they *really* are. We're quite sure we don't have any lenses on, but everyone who disagrees with us does. We're equally confident that all reasonably intelligent, honest people who have access to the same facts we do will see things just as we do. However, as we've already seen, the human brain's proclivity toward confirmation bias means we tend to ignore facts that don't comport with our preferred view of reality. Motyl also mentions the "false consensus" effect, in which we come to believe that all rational, right-thinking, well-informed people see things the way we do.

> We generate three possible explanations for why other people might not share our views: They haven't been told the truth. They are too lazy or stupid to reach correct interpretations and conclusions, or they are biased by their self-interest, dogma, or ideology....Naive realism and false consensus effects are barriers to civil political dialogue and they provide a lens through which we can better understand why liberals and conservatives seem incapable of communicating with one another without calling each other names or assuming that the other side is evil (Hitler-like, the Anti-Christ, or subhuman).[6]

Motyl concludes by providing a powerful tool for helping us break out of these dialogue-killing, empathy-destroying traps: If you find yourself in a discussion (online or otherwise) with someone who disagrees with you, "think about whether you could face that person's family over the dinner table after making your argument." He advises that if you answer "no," you may want to reconsider how you frame your argument. As I've previously noted, the anonymity and distance provided by the internet is not doing us any favors.

As University of Texas professor Michael Lind pointed out in a piece for *Tablet*, written the day after the January 6, 2020, riot at the U.S. Capitol, relationships and community are rapidly disappearing, at the cost of social stability.[7] I was in the Capitol, preparing to cast my vote on the certification of the 2020 presidential election results, when a violent mob forced its way in, resulting in the shooting death of one protester. As the rioters broke through, some members near the House chamber were quickly ushered to a secure location beneath the Capitol complex. Others were trapped inside the chamber as rioters attempted to break onto the House floor; their experience was harrowing.

While it is difficult to ascertain all their true motivations, some protestors clearly wanted to block the certification. However, even those few were not attempting to overthrow the entire government of the United States. In no way was it an "insurrection"—no one wears a buffalo hat, chaps, and little else to an insurrection. (I've seen insurgents face-to-face. I know what they look like.) The January 6 events were shameful, but so was the property destruction, violence, and lawlessness that took place in cities all across America during the summer of 2020 after a black man died while being arrested by a white police officer. The fear of rioters burning cars and buildings in your neighborhood is no less intense than that of the House members trapped on the floor with the January 6 rioters—and probably greater.

These types of events represent a preview of the grim endgame of those promoting polarization. The chaos they create, if consistent, could compel many to trade freedom for security. If we don't climb out of our information bubbles and remember how to allow people to have different views, we are in trouble. When the failure to do so is compounded by centralized power in Washington, a toxic cocktail sits ready to explode. It's also far from "we before me."

■ ■ ■

Without a doubt, we're in a precarious place. The question is, how do we find our away back from here? Some say it's impossible. Some think we're so far down the path of discord and division that the only possible outcome is the ultimate breakup of the Union that Lincoln and his generation fought, bled, and died to preserve. I don't believe that is the case. I'm holding out hope. That's why I've written this book.

It's amazing what you can do if you want something badly enough. I learned that about myself when I was in Ranger School. Everyone who goes through it suspects the COs are trying to starve them to death! You are burning an insane number of calories, yet you only get one Meal Ready to Eat in a plastic pouch each day. We were ravenously hungry all the time. By the end of the three-month course, I had lost thirty-two pounds—and I was pretty lean to begin with.

The whole point of the course is to induce massive stress and then observe your capacity to perform and lead. I vividly recall one particular February night during the desert phase of Ranger School at the Dugway proving ground in Utah. That part of the desert is barren, mountainous, and very cold in the winter. On this night, a freak thunderstorm rolled in, but with snow rather than rain. The electrical energy in it was astounding. In fact, it got so bad that the Ranger instructor said "Guys, we have to get out of here, this is unsafe." He asked who had the radio, and that happened to be me.

The instructor looked at me and said, "Okay, ranger, I want you to take out the long whip antenna and go up on top of that mountain and radio back to base that we need to be evacuated."

I looked at him and said, "Just so I'm clear, sergeant, you want me to go up on top of that hill in this lightning storm, and raise the long, metallic, whip antenna in the air, and radio for help?"

He said "Yes, ranger. And after you do that, I'll give you an extra MRE."

I said, "I'll be right back."

Needless to say, I was motivated. So, how motivated are we, as a society, to walk back from the brink of this rolling disaster of division and demonization? How hungry are we to stop thinking about people who are simply operating from a different set of assumptions as "stupid, crazy, or evil"? How badly do we want to leave a healthier social climate for our children and grandchildren?

If you're this deep into this book, I suspect you already know what I believe the larger solution to be: "we before me." But for it to work, our "we" has to extend beyond our own tribe. Toxic tribalism is a type of "we," but it's too narrow. It fuels that "us versus them" mentality. The unity that helped our great nation survive two world wars, plagues, earthquakes, hurricanes and tornados, the Great Depression, the Dust Bowl famine, 9/11 and the War on Terror, and the 2008 financial crisis is the key to surviving this crisis, too. Until we come together, this problem cannot be solved. But *when* we come together, we can solve any challenge.

This is precisely the mindset Jesus had when He told one of His most famous parables about the good Samaritan. Two thousand years later, the very phrase "good Samaritan" has become a part of our vernacular; everyone knows and understands it. What many people don't know is that Jesus offered this illustration at a time and place as polarized and tense as ours. Roman-occupied Judea was deeply fragmented along racial and sectarian religious lines. So it was no accident that the two principal characters in the story came from two groups that had generations of animosity and distrust behind them. At the heart of this timeless parable is this message: "You need a bigger 'we.'"

You and I need a bigger "we" as well. We need to be intentional about breaking out of our information bubbles so we can hear from people who view things differently than we do. We must stop letting the internet ecosystem manipulate our hearts and minds.

We need to stop attributing to our opponents the words and actions of their nuttiest, most extreme fringes. Both the left and right have fringes occupied by hateful and sometimes violent individuals. Both left and right are incentivized to score points by painting the other movement with a broad brush dipped in the extremist-fringe bucket. I'll admit I have made this mistake and recently changed my phrasing to say things like "some Democrats" or "this individual." As I've already noted, one reason our fixation on national politics has grown so all-consuming is that the power of the federal government has grown too great. It feels to everyone that there's too much at stake over which party has its hands on the levers of power in Washington, D.C., and the feds have a long-established pattern of undermining state authority. A "me first" approach assumes that I know what's best for everyone in every place. "Me first" says, "I need to take control in Washington and force my ideas on you for your own good." Top down, ideological bullying is the antithesis of "we before me." This has created a violent struggle for power in Washington that was never intended. That's why reconciling the increasingly alienated left and right in America has only one fix: rejuvenating the concept of federalism.

Federalism was the brilliant answer our nation's Founders had for the problem of uniting thirteen diverse colonies with diverging interests and attitudes. Federalism empowers the people in every state to have more real influence on the laws that govern them and thereby feel more personally powerful and less bullied by people living halfway across the country who have different values. It may not seem like it at first blush, but federalism actually advances "we before me" thinking, the opposite of the woke ideology I have described elsewhere.

The advantages to letting the states decide is that you get to have your cake and eat it, too. Under federalism, we can be the diverse America of our ideals, with each state empowered to make decisions for itself.

There are practical steps to returning power to the states. Take health care, for example. Nowhere does the Constitution grant the federal government control of our health care systems. The federal government taxes individuals and companies, and sends the proceeds back to states if they administer Medicaid and Medicare the way the federal government thinks they should (thereby evading the Tenth Amendment). And with the ideologies of the two sides so far apart, one side believes health care is a right to be provided by government; therefore, if one citizen is paying for another's health care, the patient had better not smoke! Oh, and that sugary drink and bacon are off the table, too! The other believes each individual is responsible for his own health and its care, and therefore is free to choose to live as unhealthy a lifestyle as he likes. Reconciling those ideas at the federal level violates the Constitution; it is power that rightfully resides in each state.

The final step in the process of returning power to the states is for the federal government to stop taking the money from citizens and let each state find ways to fund the necessary programs in a manner that works for it. However, getting to that point requires an intermediate step. Block grants can serve for a time to give health care dollars back to the states and let them build their Medicaid system the way they see fit.

This may be our only hope of saving the union. The anger we saw in 2020 and early 2021 has shown us that centralized power in Washington, the fight for control of that power, and the resulting tyranny of forcing one side's ideas on the other is not working.

Breaking this self-reinforcing cycle will require a critical mass of Americans from every side of our political, racial, geographical, and faith divides to stop dancing to the tune of their respective tribes and start talking to one another in a spirit of goodwill. The Samaritan was "good" because he chose to reach out to help someone his tribe told him he was supposed to hate. Layering this practice with a return to federalism will bring unity to our nation, while allowing the diversity that has so enhanced our success.

To borrow Lincoln's words, we need to choose to have malice toward none and charity for all. Let's begin the work of binding up the nation's wounds. Let's enlarge our "we" to include people who don't think like we do. We are *all* Americans. Let's put the "we" back into how we run our government and stop forcing one side's views on the other before it's too late.

CHAPTER 9

A Time for Warrior Healers

Restoration through "We Before Me"

All the greatest things are simple, and many
can be expressed in a single word: freedom; justice;
honor; duty; mercy; hope.

—Winston Churchill

As you now know, I was a soldier before I was doctor. You also know that for several remarkable years, I served first as an Army Ranger, then as both an Army and civilian physician. There's an odd contrast and tension in those two roles. A physician swears to "do no harm" to his patients; a soldier's role is to be prepared to kill if necessary. As General George Patton famously observed—with his trademark saltiness—"The object of war is not to die for your country but to make the other poor bastard die for his."[1] Of course, that is a crude oversimplification. American soldiers live (and die) by a special code of honor. They serve and are prepared to fight for noble reasons: to defend their homes and families, to protect the innocent and the vulnerable, and to serve the nation they love with a heart of gratitude for the blessing of having been born in such an extraordinary place.

Like doctors, soldiers also swear an oath: "to support and defend the Constitution of the United States against all enemies, foreign and domestic…" It surprises some to learn that our warriors don't swear to defend the people or the geography. No, they swear to defend the Constitution—or put another way, the unique idea of America.

Few of the scores of war movies made over the last 100 years have captured the essence of this, but the 2002 film *We Were Soldiers* stands as one of the few honest, honorable movies Hollywood has thus far managed to produce about the Vietnam War. The movie was an adaptation of *We Were Soldiers Once…and Young*, a remarkable 1992 book by Lt. Gen. Harold G. Moore (Ret.) and war correspondent Joseph L. Galloway chronicling their involvement in the Battle of Ia Drang, which began on November 14, 1965. In the film, Moore, who at the time was a lieutenant colonel, is played by Mel Gibson. The night before shipping out from the 7th Cavalry Regiment's battalion base overseas to South Vietnam, Moore tells the troops:

> Look around you. In the 7th Cavalry, we've got a captain from the Ukraine; another from Puerto Rico. We've got Japanese, Chinese, blacks, Hispanics, Cherokee Indians. Jews and Gentiles. All Americans. Now here in the States, some of you in this unit may have experienced discrimination because of race or creed. But for you and me now, all that is gone. We're moving into the valley of the shadow of death, where you will watch the back of the man next to you, as he will watch yours. And you won't care what color he is, or by what name he calls God. They say we're leaving home. We're going to what home was always supposed to be.
>
> Now let us understand the situation. We are going into battle against a tough and determined enemy. I can't promise

you that I will bring you all home alive. But this I swear, before you and before Almighty God, that when we go into battle, I will be the first to set foot on the field, and I will be the last to step off, and I will leave no one behind. Dead or alive, we will all come home together. So help me, God.[2]

That's not just Hollywood theatrics and good screenwriting. That is precisely the kind of commitment I saw exemplified in active war zones over and over. It is the inner heart and character I heard outwardly expressed by good men standing in harm's way—very far away from the warm comforts of home, wife, and child.

In the end, it is that idea of America that soldiers vow to defend—that any person, regardless of social, economic, ethnic, racial, or religious standing can be exactly what their effort and ability allow them to be.

There is another moment in the film that I find especially poignant. In it, the MEDEVAC helicopter pilots' CO gets into a heated exchange back at the base with a major in charge of the standard lift pilots for sending him in to evacuate the wounded in the middle of the active firefight going on in the Ia Drang Valley. The MEDEVAC pilots' furious CO yells, "Major! You called my men into a hot LZ!"

That line immediately takes me to one of the most intense and memorable nights of my military career—one in which I was on a helicopter called into a landing zone hotter than any I had ever seen and rarely heard about.

■ ■ ■

I was in Baghdad on Halloween night in 2003. We had not yet acquired the Ace of Spades, and many special operations teams from both the U.S. and our coalition partners were busy collecting other cards in the deck. That evening, the compound started buzzing that some juicy intel had just come in.

According to some of our side's electronic ears, thirteen or fourteen visiting jihadis from Sudan had called home the previous day, telling their loved ones goodbye. The clear implication was that some sort of large-scale suicide mission was about to go down. Through classified electronic wizardry, we were able to pinpoint their locations. So a combination of the U.S. Delta Force elite counterterrorism ground units and the A-Squadron of the British SAS was immediately tasked with taking them out before they got a chance to meet the seventy-two virgins promised to them in Paradise. The Night Stalkers would serve as the third leg of this triad by providing the transportation in and out, as well as the close air support.

It was clear to our intelligence folks on the ground that Iraq had become a haven for cells of several foreign terrorist networks, which was one of the now largely forgotten reasons we invaded Iraq. The media and President Bush's opponents in Congress had expressed a lot of skepticism about this, so capturing a large group of foreign jihadists would serve as smoking-gun evidence for that part of the rationale.

The target was roughly a forty-five-minute flight from Baghdad. Mike—a seasoned, first-rate medic assigned to the Delta Force squadron—and I would provide medical coverage on an MH-60K Black Hawk. The plan, as usual, was for us to stand by on a friendly helipad located a quick hop from the target. We also had two armed "Little Birds" as escorts that could provide close air support to the shooters on the target if required.

The plan that night called for several discrete teams deploying across a large compound containing four buildings. So as darkness descended, we stood by with the aircraft cranked and blades turning.

In the past, most of those missions had proven to be anticlimactic. Our guys tended to get in, get their jobs done, and get out without taking casualties.

This, tragically, would not be one of those nights.

As Mike and I sat on the flight pad, passing the time with casual conversation about the latest news from home, I noticed a rocket streak into the sky, followed by some tracer rounds. I pointed and shouted, "Did anybody else see that?" Before anyone could answer, our radio came alive with a transmission from the SAS medic, repeated several times, declaring they had casualties.

Within seconds, we were airborne and headed for the target. Some additional communication revealed there were four casualties, and one was a head wound.

The SAS guys had been tasked with breaching and clearing a key building in the compound. Per standard procedure, they'd blown open a door with a breach charge and entered the building—but the bad guys had left behind an explosive charge and remotely detonated it as soon as the first SAS guy went through the door. He took the brunt of the explosion in the face. The three guys behind him absorbed an unhealthy dose of shrapnel, and one of them also took a bullet to the pelvic region.

As soon as we took off, the pilots began discussing with the ground personnel where we would land to pick up our patients while Mike and I got our medical gear ready to treat them. This meant opening IV fluid bags, connecting the tubing, and laying out a wide array of other equipment and supplies we anticipated needing based on the types of injuries we'd been told to expect. We could do this in the dark (in fact, we were doing it in the dark) while in a bucking aircraft pitching its way through a storm and wearing full chemical/biological protective suits. We'd practiced it and done it in real situations countless times.

We were advised that we'd be setting down in the middle of an active firefight. This was not unusual for Night Stalker pilots and crew. Their very job description involves inserting and extracting special operators into and out of some of the hairiest situations imaginable. It was, however, an unusual thing for me. These elite shooters generally try to keep the doctor they're counting on to save them out of the shooting. That wasn't going to be an option this night.

The British poet Samuel Johnson is famously said to have quipped, "Nothing concentrates the mind so wonderfully as the knowledge that one is going to be hanged in the morning."[3] Winston Churchill, one of my heroes, might have had that line in mind when he, a combat veteran himself, said, "Nothing in life is so exhilarating as to be shot at without result."[4] Let me just say that as the firefight came into sight, my mind was quite concentrated.

As we slid into the landing zone, the good guys were placing heavy suppressive fire on a building about 100 feet from where we were touching down to cover our landing. About that time, one of our Bradley fighting vehicles on the opposite side of the building fired an anti-tank missile at it. However, the missile went high and streaked ridiculously close to our spinning blades. At that point, I experienced the exhilaration Churchill described.

As the helo touched down, Mike immediately jumped out and began searching for targets on the building. Meanwhile, the suppressive fire was ricocheting off the concrete building and flying all around us and into the chopper.

We expected to see the wounded heading our way the instant we landed, but we didn't. So we waited. As we sat in that awkward, vulnerable position, each second felt like a full minute. Finally, we got another call from the SAS medic in the building; he wasn't ready to load the patients yet. With one voice, the entire Night Stalker flight crew yelled something along the lines of, "So why the [bleep] are we sitting here?"

Our pilot quickly "un-assed" the area. (That's unofficial Army slang meaning, "Get the heck out of Dodge!") Instantly, we headed to an aerial release point to do racetracks in the sky until the Brits told us their guys were ready to load.

We would soon learn that the delay was due to the heroic medic on the ground valiantly fighting to save the life of the SAS soldier who'd gone through the door first. Getting four casualties packaged for transport is not easy under the best of conditions, but in the middle of a large-scale firefight, it becomes exponentially more difficult. We weren't happy, but we understood.

Helicopters are particularly vulnerable to enemy fire when landing or taking off—elevated, exposed, and moving slowly. So we were all grateful to see a good friend of mine, Dave, flying a well-armed AH-6 Little Bird, make an up-close-and-personal gun run on the building just as we lifted off. He was protecting us. We knew Dave could hit a gnat flying fifty miles per hour while in a dive with his Little Bird's .50-caliber machine gun, so despite the close proximity, no one on our side was concerned about him. Dave eventually would be awarded the Distinguished Service Medal—the nation's second-highest honor (after the Congressional Medal of Honor) for an act of extraordinary bravery under intense enemy fire—later in the war.

About ten minutes and a few laps around that invisible racetrack in the sky later, the Brits called us back to the target. As we touched down amidst a hail of tracer rounds, we could make out the silhouettes of five men: two had wounded over their shoulders, and another was hobbling on his own power toward us. We asked via radio where our fourth patient was, and were told the man who had taken the blast to the face had died. As soon as the battle was won and the surviving terrorists were in custody, his body was driven to a medical facility and handled with appropriate honors and reverence.

Meanwhile, Mike and I had three patients who needed immediate help. Two had multiple shrapnel wounds to the extremities. The third also had shrapnel wounds, but his most pressing problem was a gunshot wound (GSW) high in the upper thigh, near the pelvis. Mike took the first two, and I took the GSW. My initial concern upon examining the patient was the lack of an exit wound—meaning there was a high possibility that the bullet had traversed the pelvis, severing arteries. The worst-case scenario would be a severed femoral artery, one of the largest arteries in the body. A person with a damaged femoral can bleed out in minutes, but because the blood can collect in the pelvic cavity, there might be little to no outward evidence of it.

I was encouraged to see that my patient was conscious, alert, and talking. I stuck a wad of Kerlix—a special type of bandage—into the entry wound and then placed an IV in his arm, running a liter of normal saline wide open, then pushed ten milligrams of morphine, followed by an antibiotic. In civilian emergency rooms at that time, antibiotics were not routinely given when a patient presented with a GSW, but we often did that on the battlefield because of the nature of the environment. This brave Briton had a very serious injury, and I was certain he did not want an infection, particularly one anywhere near his private parts. Those few hours were some of the most memorable of my entire military career. Like a lot of retired soldiers, I'm not prone to talking about my decorations or awards outside the circles of people who were there. However, my congressional bio does reveal that I've received the Bronze Star and other awards. While the Bronze Star is a higher-ranking combat medal, I regard it as less than the Air Medal with "V" Device—for valor "under heavy enemy fire"—I received for my actions that night.

■ ■ ■

I mention those awards now only to provide some evidence that my life's path has afforded me the opportunity to think long and hard about this warrior-healer contrast. I think we need a lot more people serving in this role at this crossroads moment in our nation.

You may now better understand what I mean when I say I am two guys. I am half an infantry officer and Army Ranger, and half a physician who recently became a politician. I was trained to fight, then I was trained to heal. This equipped me to fight for the health and wellbeing of those entrusted to my care. And often it is, indeed, a fight. Sickness, disease, syndromes, and injuries are all pitiless enemies. They will take down everyone they can without mercy, as COVID-19 has shown us.

Today, I have a new patient. It's our society; our culture; our wonderful nation. And we're unwell. We're suffering from multiple fractures of our communities along racial, demographic, and geographic lines. Toxic infections of fear, arrogance, and entitlement are all spreading through our entire body politic, streaming via digital arteries and electronic media veins. Over the last couple of years, these infections have produced an ongoing series of seizures and convulsions that threaten to tear the body apart.

We need more warrior-healers. We need men and women willing to fight, not against their fellow Americans, but against ideas that are harmful to freedom. The distinction is critical. We need warrior-healers who put power and position last and the health of our great nation first—good people who will expand their "we" beyond their own narrow tribes, and then go to battle for that larger "we." This will require spending less time listening to the latest internet conspiracy theory and more time listening to people who don't see things the way we do. This will require spending less time on social media and more time in our neighborhoods. This will require us to stand up to cancel culture and openly express our views, regardless of the cost.

The weapons of our warfare in this fight are empathy, relational investment, a skill for speaking the truth in love, leading through serving, determined selflessness, integrity, courage, a listening spirit, grace, and virtue. But make no mistake, it will require a fight. Healing always does. We will have to fight for our families; our overregulated businesses; our polarized communities; our corrupt and decaying institutions; and those who, for several generations now, have been unfathered and under-fathered and spoon-fed a steady diet of fear, bitterness, and entitlement.

Sometimes you have to fight to get over the bridge of disillusionment. Sometimes you have to heal wounds. And our times call for a lot of both those things.

Our healing will not manifest from the top down. Getting the right people into the most powerful positions will not heal what ails us. We've seen that. Our renewal of health will only come from the bottom up. It will start with regular Americans living regular "we before me" lives.

I've tried to live this out in our nation's capital. In Washington, events very rarely involved members of both parties, so while I was campaigning for my first term, I began sharing an idea that would later become the Reagan-O'Neill Club.

I named it that because during the Reagan administration, the Republican president and Democrat Speaker of the House, Tip O'Neill, frequently sparred during the day, but a healthy relationship and shared love of Irish whiskey in the evenings helped them accomplish good things for the American people. Congresswoman Haley Stevens—a Democrat from Detroit, Michigan—agreed to help me start the club. She invited eight Democrats, and I invited eight Republicans. We insisted no policy could be discussed during our meetings; we could only share our own stories or ask about someone else's.

The club stuttered along at first; I was discouraged and nearly threw in the towel. But when Russia invaded Ukraine in early 2022, I, serving as the ranking Republican, was part of a congressional delegation led by Democrat Stephen Lynch. Stephen and I worked well together, but there were other Democrats on the trip about whom I had reservations. That said, when you're caged in a military aircraft and riding buses to refugee camps in Poland and Moldova, you cannot help but get to know people. As we all shared our stories, friendships began. I learned one of my Democrat colleagues had started a successful consulting business, and the other had launched several farm-to-table restaurants. As a businessman who knows how difficult it is to build something from nothing, I began to respect them. I was never going to agree with them on some issues, but who they were as people began to matter to me, and they felt the same about me.

But the real switch that flipped to renew my push for the Reagan-O'Neill Club came during a moment of disagreement on policy. While riding the bus to an event, I heard one of the Democrats voice a position I really disagreed with—but I realized that if I refused to listen to her, I was really refusing to listen to the seven hundred and sixty thousand Americans who had sent her to Congress. As someone who's been to combat and wrestled with giving my life for my country, I couldn't stomach that thought—so I renewed my commitment to make the club successful.

Soon after returning from the Ukraine, we relaunched the club. Now we are up to twenty-five Republicans and twenty-five Democrats, with others asking to join. We still do not discuss policy, although some people would like to. The goal is to build relationships that dial down rhetoric and can lead to reconciliation. Note I did not say "agreement": We don't have to agree; we just have to keep working together for the good of our greater "we"—the people of America.

The tool to combat the media-fueled rhetoric in today's political division is the basic principle of living a "we before me" life: strategic empathy. Nashville experienced the unthinkable in early 2023 when a transitioning transgender female opened fire on a Christian school, killing six people—three of whom were nine-year-old children. As it invariably does, this horrible act surfaced one of the most divisive debates in our country, perhaps second only to abortion: gun control. The name-calling quickly began, and there was even a heated altercation between Democrats and Republicans in the Capitol Building, just outside the U.S. House chambers.[5]

In a speech on the House floor, a Democrat who belongs to our club said Republicans are cowards for not addressing the issue, and banning weapons is the solution. Her emotional speech was filled with anguish at what has become one of America's greatest challenges: mass shootings.

Having someone who's never served in the military or law enforcement call you a coward after you've been shot at multiple times defending the country in combat will infuriate anyone, including me. For several hours I processed my emotions, and some of my instincts were to attack back. But because I had gotten to know this Democrat in the confines of the Reagan O'Neill Club, I recalled that she had a nine-year-old daughter—the exact age as the three children killed in Nashville. I began to think about what it must be like for my colleague to process what had happened.

Empathy is placing yourself in someone else's shoes to understand their perspectives. In *To Kill a Mockingbird*, Atticus Finch tells his daughter: "You never really understand a person until you consider things from his point of view... Until you climb inside of his skin and walk around in it."[6] For example, when a child scuffs a knee and screams at the top of his lungs, we can empathize by recognizing this might very well be the hardest thing that kid has ever experienced. Taken in that context, an adult can imagine their worst injury and at least empathize when someone across the aisle is doing something similar. Empathy does not mean enabling or agreeing, but that is a discussion for another book.

As I considered the raw emotion of being called a coward, I recalled when my son was diagnosed with cancer. Mitchell was only four years old at the time, and the thought of losing him created tremendous fear for me and Camie. When I've been emotional, I haven't always said the right things. I drew on those feelings as the Democrat and I sat down to talk things out later.

It is clear the two political sides have opposite solutions for the issue of gun violence in America: The left wants to ban certain weapons and restrict access for certain groups, and those on the right contend that guns protect good people from bad people with guns. Clearly, the bad guys are not following the law, and outlawing drugs has certainly not taken them off the streets. The left wants to take guns away from law-abiding citizens; those on the right encourage people to own guns and use them to protect themselves and others.

The fact that people with different views are promoting different solutions to a problem does not make those on one side cowards or those on the other something else. My Democrat colleague and I listened to one another. It was amicable, and neither of us called each other names. Did having that conversation help? It must have, because that Democrat asked me to speak at an event with business leaders from her district she'd invited to Washington for a conference on issues facing Congress, and I asked her to endorse this book. I still do not accept my colleague's solutions to the problem of gun control (Finland has as many guns per capita as the U.S. but has had zero school shootings in twenty-one years).[7] Nor does she accept mine, but the rhetoric was cooled and the relationship saved. And that could lead to dialogue that works to solve many problems.

I recently spoke to a group of students at the University of Tennessee's Baker Center, named for U.S. Senator Howard Baker, a political icon in our state. Baker was known as one who built bridges across partisan divides during his years in Congress. I talked about the political divide in America and the Reagan-O'Neill Club. The response was overwhelming, and the students asked if they could start a chapter. Congressman Blake Moore from Utah recently received a similar request when he spoke about the club at a university in his home state as well. Hopefully, we will soon have several college chapters of the club. It seems the country is hungry for "we before me."

I am a conservative, with deeply held beliefs about strictly interpreting the Constitution. That's the warrior in me. I won't back down on those. At the same time, the healer in me sees the divide itself as a major problem for our country; the tribalism is real. The Reagan-O'Neill Club is the healer in me making an effort to lead all of us to step out of our echo chambers, live the strategic empathy of "we before me," and save us from division. Haley Stevens and the other forty-eight current members of the club are warrior-healers as well.

And yet, we still need more.

CHAPTER 10

That Last Full Measure of Devotion

The Price of "We Before Me"

Greater love has no one than this, than to lay down one's life for his friends.

—Jesus of Nazareth (John 15:13 NKJV)

It's a heck of a thing to know you're about to be part of the worst day someone has ever had or likely ever will have. On a cold winter night in 2003, I felt that weight.

My assignment that night was to help inform a young widow that her husband, the father of her young children, would not be coming home.

The Night Stalkers are more than an elite regiment serving our nation's most elite warriors. They are a small, close-knit community—a family. Everyone knows everyone else. On your first day with the 160th, your spouse is asked to list four close friends or family who will serve as their support network should you be killed performing your duties. That will get your attention.

On January 30, I was still fairly new to the 160th SOAR and settling in at the regiment's headquarters in Fort Campbell, Kentucky.

Early in the day, we learned that a Night Stalker Black Hawk heli-copter had crashed near Bagram, Afghanistan, carrying four of our guys—two pilots and two crewmen. There were no survivors.

At that news, the unit instantly launched into a meticulously planned and choreographed process. The way families are notified of their fallen soldier is sacred—a method developed over the decades of hard-won experience and drawing on painful lessons.

The movie *We Were Soldiers* vividly depicts the gut-wrenching reality of notifying wives and mothers that their darkest fears have become reality. As recently as the first battles of the Vietnam War, there was no established process in place for delivering such notifica-tions to wives or parents on a grand scale. Someone at headquarters thoughtlessly decided to let yellow taxi drivers deliver the news in the form of Western Union telegrams. Many of the young wives lived on the base, so it quickly became clear to all that the appearance of a yellow taxi in the housing area meant someone's husband wasn't coming home alive.

That was not a detail added to the script for dramatic effect. That really happened. I served with a guy whose dad was deployed in that season. As a sixth-grader living on the base at Fort Benning, Georgia, he remembered frequently seeing one of those taxi cabs driving through the gates while he was playing football in an empty lot with his friends. In those moments, every boy on the field would freeze. If the ball was in midair, it would fall to the ground, uncaught. The boys would track the vehicle to see where it would stop. The boy who lived there would burst into tears and run home. Everyone else would slowly disperse and make their way home as well.

That and other appalling incidents drove the 160th SOAR to be very intentional about handling this kind of news for our unit mem-bers' loved ones. The top priority was that the family hear it from a representative of the regiment, not through the grapevine or, God forbid, through the media. Thus, we learned if multiple individuals died in the same incident, all the notifications had to be made simultaneously. Otherwise, the friends and relatives of the first person notified would likely reach out to the other families before the official notifiers could reach them.

That brings me back to that helicopter crash in early 2003. To the fury of our commanding officer, CNN had been broadcasting a report that a special operations helicopter had gone down near Bagram, killing four. The problem with that report was that any knowledgeable person seeing it would know instantly it was a Night Stalker helo. Therefore, every Night Stalker family member would instantly become frantic with worry, wondering if their loved one was among the dead. The report disappeared for a few hours, leading us to believe that someone with clout had called CNN to buy us some time to inform the families.

I recognized one of the names on the list. It was a crew chief who had previously rotated home for a health issue. Recently, as the unit physician, I had personally certified him as fit to return to duty, and he was eager to do so. No warrior wants to be safe at home when his comrades are in a fight. Nevertheless, it was sobering to realize that my signature had sent him back into harm's way, and that the worst had happened.

As quickly as possible, eight vans were lined up, filled with chaplains and the pre-selected family support teams, and sent to the homes of people about to receive heartbreaking news. I was in one of them. I will not describe for you the events that followed—as I mentioned, they are sacred—but I will tell you that night is forever seared into my memory. I will never, not even for a moment, dismiss, disrespect, or minimize the sacrifices those families and countless others made for noble and honorable reasons—who gave what Lincoln, in his Gettysburg Address called "the last, full measure of devotion."

To the best of my ability, I, one of the living, will seek to preserve what others died to defend—or in Lincoln's words, to "be dedicated here to the unfinished work which they who fought here have thus far so nobly advanced."

■ ■ ■

I close this book on this somber note because willingly putting oneself in harm's way is the ultimate expression of "we before me." It is an extraordinary thing, and it merits our honor and respect. After all, this book is about selflessness and sacrifice for others and the team. And the fact is, my life in the armed forces gave me a front-row seat to more extraordinary acts of selflessness and sacrifice than I can recount here.

I was in Afghanistan the day Pat Tillman died. You may recall that he was a professional football player, a safety for the Arizona Cardinals. But when our nation was attacked by terrorists in 2001, twenty-five-year-old Tillman traded his shoulder pads and helmet for body armor, ultimately joining the elite Army Rangers after having already served a tour of duty in Iraq.

My crew and I were flying in an MH-47 special operations helicopter, providing the medical coverage for our task force conducting a large mission over multiple simultaneous targets in Afghanistan in April 2004. Soon after inserting a group of Navy SEALs and Army Rangers, we got a call that a wounded U.S. soldier was nearby. Our aircraft immediately diverted for that location, but before we arrived, we received word to turn around. The soldier—whom we would later learn had been a victim of friendly fire in the dense fog of war—had been pronounced "killed in action." When we got back to the rear staging area, we learned that the fallen soldier was Pat Tillman.

Tillman had it all—fame, wealth, and the lifestyle that comes with being a professional athlete. He walked away from all of that because he carried in his heart the principle of "we before me." He died in the desert of Afghanistan doing something he believed in. That's why Memorial Day is far more than just a postal holiday, and the Stars and Stripes deserves our solemn respect.

That flag means something to me. It's a reminder of what an extraordinary country those who came before have bequeathed to us. Every time I hear our national anthem, I imagine Francis Scott Key sitting in the belly of that British warship as shells fell all night on Fort McHenry during the War of 1812. I see him wondering, as the morning light dawned and the smoke cleared, if he'd see that the flag of his young nation had been lowered in defeat or retreat. I imagine the thrill of emotion that surged through him to see it still flying defiantly over the fort—the inspiration that compelled him to write "The Star-Spangled Banner." I can assure you, that flag meant something to me whenever I boarded a helicopter in Iraq or Afghanistan and saw it pinned on the ceiling of the aircraft. I stooped underneath it in the back of that MH-53 when we made our high fives after hearing that Saddam Hussein had been captured.

I'm keenly aware that some in our country today reflexively roll their eyes when guys like me talk like that. They think it's corny. Or worse, they've been taught to view love of country and appreciation of our heritage as being somehow fascistic. Our schools and universities have indoctrinated a couple of generations of Americans into a warped worldview that calls patriotism "xenophobic nationalism." What a tragedy this is.

Some mistake passion for fanaticism. Others cynically characterize commitment to the core principles that undergird Western culture as extremist, simply because they have rejected those principles. I'm passionate because the more I study history, the more I come to appreciate

what an extraordinarily special place our nation is. Few today understand how blessed we are to have had wise Founders who read and
thought deeply about both the philosophy and theology of liberty. Yes,
they were flawed and broken people, as all of us are. And yes, many
failed to fully live out the ideals they wrote into our nation's founding
documents. Yet the genius of those documents helped produce a miracle
of freedom, opportunity, and progress that obliterated the Old-World
distinctions of class and birthright. Intentionally embedded in those
documents were both the moral foundation and the means to ultimately
end the remaining vestiges of that old world, such as the cursed, ungodly
institution of slavery. It ultimately required fighting our own brothers
and spilling an ocean of blood to do so, yet we willingly did it.

The result was a society that became an unprecedented wonder
of social mobility, where the children of paupers can become titans
of industry and the grandchildren of millionaires are free to end up
in poverty if they choose the path of idleness and licentiousness. Our
top 20 percent and bottom 20 percent in wealth is constantly churning, as the poorest seize the abundant opportunities here to rise
into the middle class, and as others who succeed wildly then fail.

Yet it wasn't just our founding documents that made this miracle.
It was and is America's people, too. Wave after wave of pioneers, settlers, and craftsmen came with practically nothing but a desire for a
fresh start and the opportunity to see where their sweat and ingenuity
could take them. America became a place, not of wealth hoarding or
wealth redistribution, but of wealth creation.

This produced a nation of people willing to sacrifice, fight, and
die to oppose tyranny and oppression—as we did in two world wars
and numerous other conflicts around the world. In return, we've not
asked for land or spoils—only a place to bury our dead.

For all of these reasons, the miracle of this place has served as a
beacon of hope and inspiration to others trapped in dark, oppressive

places around the world. In the depths of the Soviet gulags, dissidents looked west and saw a vision of something better. People behind fences or living in fear in Iran, China, Cuba, and many other dictatorships around the world still look to us and hope that we'll advocate for them—or at least wish them well in their quest to have a little of what we take for granted.

What we have is too precious, too rare, too good to let it go sliding into an abyss of tribalism, polarization, and entitlement while enemies like China and Russia watch, cheer, and goad our internal factions into hating one another. The ethic of "we before me" is too deeply ingrained into my being to give up on us. Part of my "we" will always be those who gave that "last full measure of devotion" because they believed in those things, too.

That means my "we" includes Tre, a fellow Night Stalker whom I got to know while treating him and his soldiers. He was from Williamson County, Tennessee, which, coincidentally, is a part of the congressional district I represent today. Tre played a role in one of the most iconic and studied engagements in America's long involvement in Afghanistan—a Navy SEAL counterinsurgency mission called Operation Redwing. The events surrounding that operation were the focus of a bestselling 2007 book *Lone Survivor: The Eyewitness Account of Operation Redwing and the Lost Heroes of SEAL Team 10*, which was later made into the film *Lone Survivor* starring Mark Wahlberg. Anyone who has seen the film will recall that near the end, a helicopter crashes while en route to rescue a group of Navy SEALS fighting against overwhelming odds. All on board were killed. Tre was in that aircraft, along with several other friends.

A year or so after his death, something brought his face to my remembrance, and on an impulse, I pulled up Facebook to see if his account was still active. It was. The final entry on his wall was the picture of a beautiful, smiling girl, probably twelve years old, accompanied by the words "I love you and I miss you daddy." That girl is part of my "we." Her noble warrior father gave his life for our freedom. That loving daughter gave us her dad. While we often honor the memory of the fallen, we should never forget the wives, husbands, mothers, fathers, sons, and daughters who feel their loss every day for the rest of their lives.

That's why I'm so passionate about seeing our nation healed. When I consider the price of our freedom and safety, it rips my heart out to see the disdain so many have for the country. Blinded by partisanship and the culture war's polarization, they see only sincerity and passion on their side, and only extremism and fanaticism on the other. So, to my dismay, I and so many other Republicans continue to be portrayed as hateful or terrible by those who either can't or won't break out of this tribal way of thinking. And to be fair, lumping all Democrats into the America-hating crowd is equally false and damaging. The woke cancel culture is not "we before me."

I hope you now see how ironic those smears are. My fervent passion is to build bridges and fight against the dissolution of my beloved country; I hope to bring healing to our wounded, fractured culture. Because I understand what a precious gift freedom is, I'll contend with all my strength for that.

America has never been a perfect expression of her high ideals, but those ideals—freedom, equality of opportunity, a fundamental understanding of the intrinsic value of every human being—have been part of our national DNA from our beginning. Good people have died to preserve what we have and to purchase those blessings for others.

I will continue to fight for those things. I won't stop fighting for America's healing, and for the restoration of our culture, our businesses, and our families. I can't. Why?

For one thing, "Night Stalkers don't quit." Also, I've learned the transformational power of "we before me." I hope all Americans will choose to live by its power. Only by placing all of us above our individual selves will we save this great nation.

Conclusion

After these four decades then, there stands before the entire world one great and inescapable conclusion: freedom leads to prosperity. Freedom replaces the ancient hatreds among the nations with comity and peace. Freedom is the victor.... General Secretary Gorbachev, if you seek peace, if you seek prosperity for the Soviet Union and Eastern Europe, if you seek liberalization: Come here to this gate. Mr. Gorbachev, open this gate. Mr. Gorbachev, tear down this wall!

—Ronald Reagan, June 12, 1987,
Brandenburg Gate, Berlin, Germany

I recognize that I have leaned heavily on military examples and illustrations as I've attempted to mark out the "we before me" pathway back to greatness for all of us. While so many lessons began on that dirt road in Mississippi, most of my life's learning in the Army vetted and added to those lessons from my youth. It is my story. Whether in the company I started or my time in politics, the motto sewn into the lining of my 160th SOAR baseball cap has been the goal of my life and central to my success.

War tests a team like no other challenge. In life and in business, I have discovered that what works amid the "fog of war" and the chaos of the battlefield also works in less-intense contexts. These military lessons are relevant because we all, as a culture, are at war in a sense. As I said in the opening pages of the book, we're under attack, not from an external enemy but an internal one—polarization. And as a culture, to fail to fight it is to surrender to destruction.

Tier One special operations units like Delta Force and SEAL Team 6 could not function without "we before me" thinking. There are no mavericks, show-boaters, or lone wolves on a special operations team. Every individual is committed wholly and only to the wellbeing of the others and the success of the mission. Each has a role to play and brings his or her specific gifts and skills to that role.

Hopefully, I've made the case that this is the model which will carry any family, company, nonprofit organization, and our nation to restored greatness. In the aftermath of two of the most divisive and emotionally fraught elections since Lincoln's in 1860, we need a heavy dose of this approach if we are going to overcome this internal threat. The importance grows as we approach another in 2024.

The pathway back to a healthier culture can be captured in a three-word maxim even a child can grasp and say: "We before me." Determined selflessness. Honesty. Courage. Grace. Communication. Listening. Serving. Sacrifice. The critical virtues and principles of this book. It's so simple that it's easy to overlook its importance. So, along the way I have pointed to examples of that powerful principle in action, including the example of the man I admire more than any other, my father. However, there is one additional fact about his life that I have yet to share.

As I was writing this conclusion, Dad—now in his early eighties—called to tell me he finally has to hang it up. He's spent. During his life of ministry, he has often served as an interim pastor for churches.

Some needed one after they split apart or were in some other crisis due to division, strife, or financial challenges (as even churches aren't immune to the toxin of tribalism). My father stepped into those sometimes-dysfunctional communities and facilitated reconciliation and restoration. And more often than not, he did this for no salary. (Some churches in this situation struggled to find a pastor because the circumstances were so bad, no sane person would take the opening. Others simply could no longer pay a full-time pastor because the church's finances had deteriorated so badly.) The irony is clear: My one-armed dad is a physically broken man whom God has used to heal broken churches.

Invariably, as Dad steps into these congregations, he comes preaching, teaching, and modeling the same truth I learned while serving as his "right hand": The miracle cure for what ails these sickly churches is simply "we before me." That same prescription will heal our nation, propel your organization or business to the next level, and help you lead a productive and fruitful life. It's the key to greatness at every level of human endeavor. As Ralph Waldo Emerson observed, "One of the beautiful compensations of this life is that no man can sincerely help another without helping himself."[1]

When I speak at college graduations, I often observe that if the old adage that says, "the eyes of man are never satisfied" is true, then no number of degrees on the wall, awards on the shelf, or money in a bank account will ever bring happiness. The one thing that does is serving others. Nothing quenches the hunger for more like an act of unrewarded, unrecognized service. My friend Bill was right when he said the act of service is reward enough. If personal satisfaction is your goal, start there.

Like my father, I have a heart for reconciliation. I'm convinced the virtues I've championed here will go a long way toward healing our fractured society, including the racial divisions that have figured so prominently in our national discourse over the last couple of years. We've also seen that it is the abandonment of those very virtues that has amplified the disparities driving so much resentment and anger in this moment. These principles simply and quietly work.

I never fail to be moved and challenged when I read the seventeenth chapter of John. There, Christ, who has just stated plainly to His followers that He knows He is about to be arrested and killed, is praying for their unity. His final prayer reveals that He saw division as the greatest threat to their success in the mission of "going into all the world" to preach His message. The same is true for our communities and our businesses, and it is true for you as you seek to achieve your highest God-given potential. We have to put away pettiness, animosity, and the rampant "us vs. them" paradigm that dominates our current way of thinking. In my own life, especially now that I spend so much of my time in the highly polarized and contentious battlefield of our nation's capital, I frequently remind myself of the truth of other things Jesus said. Matthew records Him talking about prayer and worship; and Jesus basically says (paraphrasing), "If you come to the altar to worship with an offering, and suddenly remember that a brother or sister has something against you, stop, leave your offering there, and go be reconciled first." There's an amazing takeaway for us in that statement regarding God's priorities. The message from Christ seems to be: "God actually places a higher value on you being reconciled to others than on your worship of Him." God, too, believes in "we before me."

A few weeks after the events of January 6, 2021, one of my Democrat colleagues, Alexandria Ocasio-Cortez, made an outlandish statement suggesting that it made her afraid of all Republicans. As someone who took the oath to defend all Americans and put that oath on the line in combat, I was angry about that comment. The black former NFL player who became a pastor and now leads the Bible study in my DC home when we are in session suggested I live by the conviction from the verse above and confront AOC about it. A few days later, I saw her sitting on the floor of the House as we were voting, so I joined her and shared my frustration. I had sat next to her on the Oversight Committee a few times, and we'd had many conversations. I told her I was taken aback by her comments. I assured her I would have protected her had any crowd attempted to harm her. I also reminded her that I had been (and in my heart, still am), a soldier, willing to die to protect this country. And I said that her comment made me mad because her rationale for it was simply untrue. She grasped my forearm, and with a tear in her eye said she was deeply sorry. We talked about how damaging it is when we lump people together and agreed to not use words like "us vs. them" again.

For my part, I have tried to attack problems and not people, although at times in the political world, we have to draw contrasts between ourselves and our opponents—meaning we have to say things like, "Democrats are doing this." I have changed my language to communicate that "certain elements of the Democrats in Congress" or the "leadership of their party" are doing those things, in order to be more accurate and to give room to those Democrats who do not agree with many of their party's positions. Reconciliation as described in the above Bible verses can happen, but we will have to take baby steps before we can run.

It is not necessary to be a Christian, or even a person of faith, to embrace and benefit from the "we before me" virtues. The most confident atheist or committed agnostic can recognize their civil benefits, and indeed, many do. Prominent, outspoken atheist Sam Harris has expended significant time and effort hoping to prove that it's possible to be virtuous without believing in God. He's written an entire book attempting to make that case, *The Moral Landscape* (2010).[2] I don't find Harris's efforts to root objective morality in brain science and data all that persuasive, but the very fact that he and other atheists are making the effort testifies to the fact that they recognize how vital a common moral code is to advance both individual and societal well-being.

Thomas Jefferson also was an irreligious rationalist. His personal copy of the Bible was unique. He'd spent years cutting out all the scriptures with references to miracles or the deity of Christ with a razor blade, while leaving in the moral and ethical lessons. Why? Because he realized, correctly, that a common moral code is the glue that holds a diverse, free people together. He saw virtue as essential to liberty. He understood mankind's great propensity for evil is the pathway to tyranny. In an 1816 letter to a friend, Jefferson wrote, "[W]ithout virtue, happiness cannot be."[3] To another friend, Jefferson wrote, "Happiness [is] the aim of life. Virtue [is] the foundation of happiness."[4] Toward the end of his life, he published his personal compilation of the moral teachings of Jesus in English, French, Latin, and Greek, titled *The Life and Morals of Jesus of Nazareth*. Jefferson was likely no Christian, yet he clearly grasped the need for a moral code to hold civil society together and enable progress. He viewed the code found in the Bible as the best humanity has to offer.

Hopefully I've made the case for that "golden triangle" of virtue, freedom, and faith here. I also hope that as you've read these chapters, you've come to better understand what a precious and fragile thing freedom is, as well as the vital role the virtues to which I've pointed play in maintaining and safeguarding "liberty and justice for all." We simply can't have freedom without virtue. Not for long, anyway.

Today, the objective of freedom is, in my view, the same as it was in 1789: to enable everyone to use their gifts and abilities to make whatever they can of life, and to go as far as their effort, creativity, and diligence can take them. I am convinced this is God's original ideal for all people everywhere. Each person is a unique and remarkable work of art, a painting—and we learn about the Painter by looking at the painting. If that is true, then any system that keeps you from putting your unique gifts and abilities to work for your fulfillment, the well-being of your family, and the good of your community obscures that painting. Limiting freedom or addicting someone to a government handout equally cause people not to utilize their gifts, and that obscures the painting as well.

The Founders basically framed that same truth another way: They viewed as "self-evident" the truth that God has bestowed on all people certain "inalienable rights"—meaning rights that cannot be forfeited or stolen—and that among those are the right to "life, liberty, and the pursuit of happiness." Notice they did not suggest there is a right to happiness—rather, only the right to *pursue* it. This is a vital distinction in our day because so many seem to believe that government has an obligation to guarantee good outcomes for everyone. Indeed, it cannot, nor should it try. When government attempts to force equality of outcomes, it has to take something one person has earned and give it to someone who has not earned it—which disincentivizes making an effort and leads to an overall decrease in prosperity for all. In the end, the government is only able to take one thing from any of us to ensure such an outcome—and that is freedom.

Freedom, if it means anything at all, must mean the freedom to fail. True liberty must involve the latitude not only to make poor choices but also to live with the consequences of those choices. As great American thinker Thomas Sowell and so many others have pointed out, a free and just system should attempt to guarantee equality of opportunity for all, but cannot and should not try to guarantee equality of outcome. In a 2015 syndicated column, he wrote:

> Many in the media and among the intelligentsia are all too ready to go along, in the name of seeking equality. But equality of what? Equality before the law is a fundamental

value in a decent society. But equality of treatment in no way guarantees equality of outcomes. On the contrary, equality of treatment makes equality of outcomes unlikely, since virtually nobody is equal to somebody else in the whole range of skills and capabilities required in real life. When it comes to performance, the same man may not even be equal to himself on different days, much less at different periods of his life.[5]

In the same piece, Sowell correctly warns that the quest for this misguided, unobtainable form of "equality" will produce the very kind of identity politics, divisions, and conflicts that we've witnessed in recent years.

A confused conception of equality is a formula for never-ending strife that can tear a whole society apart—and has already done so in many countries.[6]

That warning was prophetic, don't you think?

As many other examples from history testify, it is disastrous to limit freedom in order to force equal results through the coercive power of government. Doing so not only destroys the very things that make for a prosperous society—including innovation, incentive, and entrepreneurship—but never delivers on its utopian promises. It cannot. The devil's bargain is to trade liberty for a promise of security. But as many socialist revolutions have demonstrated, once you've traded away your precious freedom, the promises of economic security prove to be just an illusion. Ask the Venezuelans fleeing the Maduro regime about that if you don't believe me. They concentrated power into the hands of one man and got a dictator. Thank God for our Founders' concept of federalism.

This is where we are, yet I'm convinced it is possible to turn our nation around—that a renaissance of freedom and respect amid differences will begin as you and I, as individuals, begin to live the "we before me" ethic and its associated virtues with our neighbors. We can then extend it to our businesses, organizations, and churches. Ultimately, we can help transform the culture in the only way lasting change is truly possible: from the bottom up.

I want to reiterate: I am not advocating agreement on the solutions. I am advocating for relationships that place the whole ahead of our own selves—relationships that can dial down the rhetoric and lead to real dialogue. Listening, and agreeing to disagree without hate, is the starting point.

Will future generations of Americans look back on us and say, "This was their finest hour"? My earnest hope is that they will. I pray that they will speak with admiration and gratitude about the way we rejected the poisonous trap of tribalism, repudiated the seductive lie of messianic government, chose virtue and self-government instead, and began to look after one another. This is the pathway to greatness and renewal for all of us.

Let's start walking it. There is no time to lose.

Notes

Introduction

1. Winston Churchill, *The Second World War: Their Finest Hour*, vol. II (Boston: Houghton Mifflin Company, 1949), 198.
2. Jack Fowler, "The War within the States," *National Review*, August 4, 1989, 35–36.
3. Peter Wood, "The Gilded Rage: Why Is America So Angry?," *The Spectator*, October 7, 2019, https://thespectator.com/uncategorized/gilded-rage-america -angry.
4. Bettina J. Casad and J. E. Luebering, "Confirmation Bias," *Encyclopedia Britannica*, October 9, 2019, https://www.britannica.com/science/confirmation -bias, accessed April 16, 2021.
5. Amy Chua, *Political Tribes: Group Instinct and the Fate of Nations* (New York: Penguin Press, 2018), 7.
6. Ibid., 12.
7. Jonah Goldberg, *Suicide of the West: How the Rebirth of Tribalism, Nationalism, and Socialism Is Destroying American Democracy* (New York: Crown Forum, 2020), ix.

Chapter 1: We Before Me: A Heritage

1. In 2020, several journalists, none of whom had ever served in the military, began to attack as dishonest Republican veteran politicians who had only graduated from Ranger School, never served in a Ranger unit, and who claimed to be "Army Rangers." The National Ranger Association responded after these politicians attacked Senator Tom Cotton, issuing a statement confirming that the definition of an "Army Ranger" was always someone who either served in an Army Ranger unit *or* had graduated from U.S. Army Ranger School. This pretty much shut up the journalists who were trying to create a fake controversy to diminish politicians they didn't like.
2. Lance Betros, *Carved from Granite: West Point Since 1902* (College Station, Texas: Texas A&M University Press, 2012), xv.
3. Rick Atkinson, *The Long Gray Line: The American Journey of West Point's Class of 1966* (London: Picador, 2010), 24.

Chapter 2: The Elusive Pea: "We Before Me" Helps Us Overcome Adversity

1. Robert H. Bork, *Slouching Towards Gomorrah: Modern Liberalism and American Decline* (New York: Harper Perennial, 2010), 11.

Chapter 3: The Golden Triangle of Freedom: The Relationship between Virtue, Faith, and Freedom

1. Francis Sempa, "Niebuhr on the Crisis of Our Civilization," Russell Kirk Center for Cultural Renewal, November 15, 2020, https://kirkcenter.org/essays/niebuhr-on-the-crisis-of-our-civilization.
2. Metaxas, in turn, credits prolific author and social critic Os Guinness with framing the concept in his sobering book, *A Free People's Suicide: Sustaining Freedom and the American Future* (Downers Grove, Illinois: IVP Press, 2012).
3. Eric Metaxas, *If You Can Keep It: The Forgotten Promise of American Liberty* (New York: Penguin Publishing Group, 2017), 54.
4. John Adams, "Letter to the Officers of the First Brigade of the Third Division of the Militia of Massachusetts (October 11, 1798)," in *The Works of John Adams, Second President of the United States*, ed. Charles Francis Adams (Boston: Little, Brown, and Company, 1854), 9:229.
5. H. A. Washington, *The Writings of Thomas Jefferson*, vol. VII (Frankfurt, Germany: Outlook Verlag, 2018), 115.
6. Guinness, *A Free People's Suicide*, 99–100.
7. James Campbell, *Recovering Benjamin Franklin: An Exploration of a Life of Science and Service* (Chicago: Open Court, 1999), 133.
8. James A. Herrick, *The Making of the New Spirituality: The Eclipse of the Western Religious Tradition* (Downers Grove, Illinois: InterVarsity Press, 2004), 76.
9. Benjamin Franklin to Ezra Stiles, March 9, 1790 in *Works of Benjamin Franklin*, ed. John Bigelow (New York: G. P. Putnam and Sons, 1904), 185.
10. Ronald Reagan, "January 5, 1967: Inaugural Address (Public Ceremony)," Ronald Reagan Presidential Library and Museum, https://www.reaganlibrary.gov/archives/speech/january-5-1967-inaugural-address-public-ceremony.
11. Paul Harvey, *Remember These Things* (Washington, D.C.: Heritage Foundation, 1952), 72–73.
12. Ibid., 31.

Chapter 4: Absolute Power Corrupts Absolutely: A Society without "We Before Me"

1. "List of Saddam's Crimes Is Long," ABC News, December 30, 2006, https://abcnews.go.com/WNT/IraqCoverage/story?id=2761722&page=1.
2. Ibid.
3. UNAMI, "Disputed Internal Boundaries: Sheikhan District," vol. 1, 2009, 2–3.

4. "List of Saddam's Crimes Is Long."
5. "The Iraqi Government Assault on the Marsh Arabs," Human Rights Watch, January 25, 2003, https://www.hrw.org/report/2003/01/25/iraqi-government -assault-marsh-arabs.
6. Ibid.
7. Dilshad Anwar and Rikar Hussein, "Iraq Unearths Mass Graves Believed to Contain Kurds Slain in 1987–88," VOA, July 25, 2019, https://www.voanews.com /extremism-watch/iraq-unearths-mass-graves-believed-contain-kurds-slain-1987 -88.
8. United States Department of Defense, "Environmental Exposure Report: Oil Well Fires," GulfLINK, last updated October 13, 1998, https://gulflink.health.mil /oil_well_fires/index.html.
9. Hosny Khordagui and Dhari Al-Ajmi, "Environmental Impact of the Gulf War: An Integrated Preliminary Assessment," *Environmental Management* 17, no. 4 (1993): 557–62, https://link.springer.com/article/10.1007/BF02394670.
10. Jennifer Rosenberg, "Crimes of Saddam Hussein," ThoughtCo., updated December 31, 2018, https://www.thoughtco.com/the-war-crimes-of-saddam -hussein-721494.
11. Jonah Goldberg, *Suicide of the West* (New York: Crown Forum, 2018), 49.

Chapter 5: Until They Know How Much You Care: How "We Before Me" Can Empower Your Company

1. Gen. Stanley McChrystal et al., *Team of Teams: New Rules of Engagement for a Complex World* (New York: Portfolio Penguin, 2015), 2.
2. Bob Boylan, *Get Everyone in Your Boat Rowing in the Same Direction: 5 Leadership Principles to Follow So Others Will Follow You* (Coon Rapids, Minnesota: Adams Media Corp, 1995), 18.
3. The Align MD Culture Statement reads:

    Motto of the Align MD Culture:

    "We before me"

    Culture Statements:

    The Emergency Department Team

    A. I will never say a negative comment about an emergency department team member without first addressing the issue to the individual and his or her leader.

    B. I will do my best to cover shifts for colleagues when they ask and will never abuse this commitment from others for my selfish gain.

    C. I will always be on time for a shift and, if late, will call to notify the team no later than ten minutes after the start of my shift.

    D. I will be honest with everyone.

    E. Understanding that when I speak to someone on the medical staff I am a representative of the entire ED team, I will always have the patient fully worked up and be prepared to answer all questions of the admitting physician prior to calling.

F. I will never use the words, "I don't know," but will at a minimum say, "Let me find out for you."

G. I accept diversity among team members and patients.

H. Because I want to be better tomorrow than I am today, I thrive on the input of others and seek it as much as possible.

I. I will always give 100 percent for every hour of every shift.

J. I will comply with the requirements of my partner hospital.

The Patient

A. I will put the clinical and service care of the patient over everything else.

B. I will smile with every patient and introduce myself to every person in the room with the patient.

C. I will thank every patient for allowing us to take care of him or her.

D. Except when clinically impossible, I will sit down in the room when collecting data.

E. I will ensure the patient knows that myself and the patient are a team making decisions together about their care.

F. I will always close the encounter with the patient [by] giving them the results, diagnosis, and next recommended actions.

G. I accept that patients are uneducated about their disease, creating fear. I am often treating fear more than I treat disease.

4. Paul Martinelli, "What Is a Servant Leader?," John Maxwell Team, 2019, http://cdn1.johnmaxwellteam.com/cds/marketing/digital_products/JMT-WhatIsAServantLeader.pdf.

5. The DiSC Personality Profile is owned by Personality Profile Solutions, LLC. More information is available at https://www.discprofile.com/what-is-disc.

6. Gallup, Inc. is a data analytics company that developed the StrengthsFinder system. More information is available at https://www.gallup.com/cliftonstrengths/en/strengthsfinder.aspx.

7. Sam Dorman, "Virginia Moving to Eliminate All Accelerated Math Courses before 11th Grade as Part of Equity-Focused Plan," Fox News, April 22, 2021, https://www.foxnews.com/us/virginia-accelerated-math-courses-equity.

8. Marshall Fishwick, ed., *Ronald Revisited: The World of Ronald McDonald* (Bowling Green, Kentucky: Bowling Green University Popular Press, 1983), 110.

Chapter 6: Toward a More Perfect Union: How "We Before Me" Can Rescue Our Families

1. "Whatever It Takes," Genius, June 18, 2007, https://genius.com/Lifehouse-whatever-it-takes-lyrics.

2. Les Parrott and Leslie Parrott, *Saving Your Marriage Before It Starts: Seven Questions to Ask Before—and After—You Marry* (Grand Rapids, Michigan: Zondervan, 2015), 11.

3. Greg Smalley, "Are You a Selfish Spouse?," Focus on the Family, October 31, 2017, https://www.focusonthefamily.com/marriage/how-to-fight-selfishness-in-marriage.
4. Ibid.
5. "The Negro Family: The Case for National Action," United States Department of Labor, March 1965, https://www.dol.gov/general/aboutdol/history/webid-moynihan.
6. James Q. Wilson, "Why We Don't Marry," *City Journal*, Winter 2002, https://www.city-journal.org/article/why-we-dont-marry.
7. Elizabeth Wildsmith, Jennifer Manlove, and Elizabeth Cook, "Dramatic Increase in the Proportion of Births outside of Marriage in the United States from 1990 to 2016," Child Trends, August 8, 2018, https://www.childtrends.org/publications/dramatic-increase-in-percentage-of-births-outside-marriage-among-whites-hispanics-and-women-with-higher-education-levels.
8. Ibid.
9. W. Bradford Wilcox and Wendy Wang, "The Marriage Divide: How and Why Working-Class Families Are More Fragile Today," Institute for Family Studies, September 25, 2017, https://ifstudies.org/blog/the-marriage-divide-how-and-why-working-class-families-are-more-fragile-today.
10. Wilson, "Why We Don't Marry."
11. Mary Eberstadt, "Two Nations, Revisited," *National Affairs*, Summer 2018, https://www.nationalaffairs.com/publications/detail/two-nations-revisited.
12. Cynthia Harper and Sara S. McLanahan, "Father Absence and Youth Incarceration," *Journal of Research on Adolescence* 14, no. 3 (September 2004): 369–97, https://doi.org/10.1111/j.1532-7795.2004.00079.x.
13. Timothy S. Goeglein and Craig Osten, *American Restoration: How Faith, Family, and Personal Sacrifice Can Heal Our Nation* (Washington, D.C.: Regnery Gateway, 2019), citing M. Myers, "Fatherless Daughters: How Growing Up without a Dad Affects Women," Medium, June 14, 2021, https://medium.com/daughters-without-dads-being-emotionally-or/fatherless-daughters-how-growing-up-without-a-dad-affects-women-eabcedfd09c8.
14. Goeglein and Osten, *American Restoration*, citing Suzanne Venker, "Missing Fathers and America's Broken Boys—The Vast Majority of Mass Shooters Come from Broken Homes," Fox News, February 19, 2018, https://www.foxnews.com/opinion/missing-fathers-and-americas-broken-boys-the-vast-majority-of-mass-shooters-come-from-broken-homes.
15. Goeglein and Osten, *American Restoration*, citing Nicholas Zill, "Substance Abuse, Mental Illness, and Crime More Common in Disrupted Families," Institute for Family Studies, March 24, 2015, https://ifstudies.org/blog/substance-abuse-mental-illness-and-crime-more-common-in-disrupted-families.
16. "Poverty Status of Children by Family Structure, 2021," U.S. Department of Justice, OJJDP Statistical Briefing Book, https://ojjdp.ojp.gov/statistical-briefing

-book/population/faqs/qa01203#:~:text=In%202021%2C%209.5%25%20of %20children,17.4%25).

17. Glenn T. Stanton, "The Research Proves the No. 1 Social Justice Imperative Is Marriage," *The Federalist*, November 3, 2017, https://thefederalist.com/2017/11 /03/research-proves-no-1-social-justice-imperative-marriage.

18. Scott Yenor, "The True Origin of Society: The Founders on the Family," Heritage Foundation, October 16, 2013, https://www.heritage.org/political-process/report/ the-true-origin-society-the-founders-the-family.

19. Goeglein and Osten, *American Restoration*, 59.

20. Timothy P. Carney, "Failing Families," *Washington Examiner*, June 26, 2018, https://www.washingtonexaminer.com/opinion/american-culture-is-moving-into -a-post-family-era.

21. Goeglein and Osten, *American Restoration*, 61, referencing Wilson, "Why We Don't Marry."

Chapter 7: To Cross the Great Divide: "We Before Me" Can Unite Our Nation

1. Abigail Thernstrom and Stephan Thernstrom, "Black Progress: How Far We've Come, and How Far We Have to Go," Brookings Institute, March 1, 1998, https://www.brookings.edu/articles/black-progress-how-far-weve-come-and -how-far-we-have-to-go.

2. Kevin McCaffree and Anondah Saide, "How Informed Are Americans about Race and Policing?," Civil Unrest and Presidential Election Study 007, Skeptic Research Center, February 20, 2021, https://www.skeptic.com/research-center/reports/ Research-Report-CUPES-007.pdf.

3. "Our Changing Population: United States," USA Facts, last updated July 2022, https://usafacts.org/data/topics/people-society/population-and-demographics/our -changing-population.

4. "Expanded Homicide Data Table 6," Crime in the U.S. 2019, FBI Uniform Crime Report, https://ucr.fbi.gov/crime-in-the-u.s/2019/crime-in-the-u.s.-2019/tables/ expanded-homicide-data-table-6.xls.

5. Abdul Rad, "Police Institutions and Police Abuse: Evidence from the US," (master's thesis, Oxford University, Department of Politics and International Relations, 2019), http://dx.doi.org/10.2139/ssrn.3246419.

6. Samantha Michaels, "Police Unions Have Enormous War Chests to Defend Officers Like Derek Chauvin," *Mother Jones*, March 19, 2021, https://www .motherjones.com/crime-justice/2021/03/police-unions-have-enormous-war-chests -to-defend-officers-like-derek-chauvin; Derek Hawkins, "Officer Charged in George Floyd's Death Used Fatal Force Before and Had History of Complaints," *Washington Post*, May 29, 2020, https://www.washingtonpost.com/nation/2020 /05/29/officer-charged-george-floyds-death-used-fatal-force-before-had-history -complaints.

Chapter 8: The Rest of the Story: How "We Before Me" Works across All Divisive Issues

1. Matt Motyl, "Liberals and Conservatives Are (Geographically) Dividing" in P. Valdesolo and J. Graham eds., *Social Psychology of Political Polarization*, Bridging Ideological Divides: The Claremont Symposium for Applied Social Psychology (Sage Press, 2014), 6.

2. Paul Barrett, Justin Hendrix, and Grant Sims, "How Tech Platforms Fuel U.S. Political Polarization and What Government Can Do about It," Brookings Institute, September 27, 2021, https://www.brookings.edu/blog/techtank/2021/09/27/how-tech-platforms-fuel-u-s-political-polarization-and-what-government-can-do-about-it.

3. Hunt Allcot et al., "The Welfare Effects of Social Media," *American Economic Review* 110, no. 3 (March 2020): 629–76, https://www.aeaweb.org/articles?id=10.1257/aer.20190658.

4. Jonah Berger and Katherine L. Milkman, "What Makes Online Content Viral?," *Journal of Marketing Research* 49, no. 2 (2012): 192–205, http://jonahberger.com/wp-content/uploads/2013/02/ViralityB.pdf.

5. Daniel Lattier, "The Media Needs to Keep You Angry. Don't Feed into It," FEE Stories, January 23, 2019, https://fee.org/articles/the-media-needs-to-keep-you-angry-dont-feed-into-it.

6. Matt Motyl, "If You Don't Agree with Me, There's Something Wrong with You," Civil Politics, https://www.civilpolitics.org/content/if-you-dont-agree-me-there-something-wrong-you-introduction-naive-realism.

7. Michael Lind, "The Five Crises of the American Regime," *Tablet*, January 7, 2021, https://www.tabletmag.com/sections/news/articles/american-crises-capitol-assault.

Chapter 9: A Time for Warrior Healers: Restoration through "We Before Me"

1. Carlo D'Este, *Patton: Genius for War* (New York: HarperCollins, 1996), 1.

2. *We Were Soldiers*, directed by Randall Wallace (Paramount Pictures, 2002).

3. This is actually a commonly shared and cited paraphrase of Johnson's words. The actual quote, according to his biographer James Boswell, was, "Depend upon it, sir, when a man knows he is to be hanged in a fortnight, it concentrates his mind wonderfully." Ralph Keyes, *The Quote Verifier: Who Said What, Where, and When* (New York: St. Martin's Press, 2007), 35.

4. Winston Churchill, *The Story of the Malakand Field Force: An Episode of Frontier War* (London: Longmans, Green, 1898), 172.

5. Stephen Collinson, "A Tense Exchange on Capitol Hill That Perfectly Captures America's Divide on Guns," CNN, March 30, 2023, https://www.cnn.com/2023/03/30/politics/american-gun-divide-nashville/index.html.

6. Harper Lee, *To Kill A Mockingbird* (New York: Grand Central Publishing, 1960), 39.

7. "Interestingly, European societies that come close to US rates of gun ownership, in terms of gun owners per 100 people, (but with hunting rifles and shotguns rather than handguns), such as Finland and Norway, are among the safest societies internationally with regards to gun violence." Peter Squires, "U.S. Shootings: Norway and Finland Have Similar Levels of Gun Ownership, but Far Less Crime," The Conversation, May 27, 2022, https://theconversation.com/us-shootings-norway-and-finland-have-similar-levels-of-gun-ownership-but-far-less-gun-crime-183933.

Conclusion

1. Daniel Coenn, *Ralph Waldo Emerson: His Words* (München, Germany: BookRix, 2014), 12.
2. "People who do not believe in God or an afterlife, and yet still think it important to subscribe to a religious tradition, only believe this because living this way seems to make some positive contribution to their well-being or to the well-being of others." Sam Harris, *The Moral Landscape: How Science Can Determine Human Values* (New York: Free Press, 2011), 33.
3. Thomas Jefferson to Amos J. Cook, January 21, 1816, Founders Online, https://founders.archives.gov/documents/Jefferson/03-09-02-0243.
4. Thomas Jefferson to William Short, October 31, 1819, Founders Online, https://founders.archives.gov/documents/Jefferson/03-15-02-0141-0001.
5. Thomas Sowell, "The 'Equality' Racket," Creators.com, January 6, 2015, https://www.creators.com/read/thomas-sowell/01/15/the-equality-racket.
6. Ibid.